# ALL-STEEL TRAVELLER

## NEW & SELECTED POEMS

## PAMELA GILLILAN

G000243983

## BLOODAXE BOOKS

First published 1994 by
Bloodaxe Books Ltd,
P.O. Box 1SN,
Newcastle upon Tyne NE99 1SN.


Bloodaxe Books Ltd acknowledges
the financial assistance of Northern Arts.

Cover printing by J. Thomson Colour Printers Ltd, Glasgow.

Printed in Great Britain by
Cromwell Press Ltd, Broughton Gifford, Melksham, Wiltshire.

'It may be there is no place for any of us. Except we know there is, somewhere; and if we found it, but lived there only a moment, we could count ourselves blessed. This could be your place,' he said, shivering as though in the sky spreading wings had cast a cold shade. 'And mine.'

TRUMAN CAPOTE, *The Grass Harp* (1951)


each day's skin
stitched to another day's drum

KEN SMITH, *Hawkwood* (1986)

# Acknowledgements

This book includes poems reprinted from Pamela Gillilan's first collection, *That Winter* (Bloodaxe Books, 1986). Seven poems appeared in *Travelling the Worlds*, with Peter Dent (Spacex Literature, 1992). Acknowledgements are due to the editors of the following publications in which some of the other poems first appeared: *Aberystwyth Poetry Competition Anthology* (1994), *Heritage Poets Anthology, Orbis, Oxford Poetry, South West Poetry Competition Anthology* (1991), *Ver Verse, Vision On, Westwords,* and *York & District Anthology* (1990). 'Crystal Set' was broadcast by BBC Radio 4.

# Contents

**4 DRIVING TO THE LAKE**

# 1  ARM IN ARM

# Journey

It was new to see the dark. All the shops
had lights; in front of each
flat gardens of light lay on the pavement.
The tram swung along.

There is no sound in this memory,
no clank of tram, though the tram sways.
No talk. What kind of words would she be saying?
Her mouth moves around words. Her body
flings and fidgets, restless
with the excitement
of darkness and yellow light.
A varnished bench
follows the rounded
panels and windows
of the tram's deck.
She kneels on the seat, stares
out of the curve of glass
downward and backward
along thin steely tracks.

I can see her father now; can nearly see him.
He seems a calm young man,
overcoated, blond and broad.
He is her steadiness.
She is not old enough to wonder,
to need a reason for the outing.
She falls asleep against his tweed.

She is in his arms. They enter
the passage of the narrow house.
The slender hands of maiden great-aunts
flutter in welcome. She sways
between the soft brownness of their skirts.

In the Victorian dimness
flat white towels on a rail,
high soft bed that is not hers,
her father hurrying away.

# East Finchley

In London's winter darkness by tea-time;
crumpets toasted by the fire, and chestnuts.
We picked jewels from the bitter cells of pomegranates
and one year there was a glut of sweet green grapes
dusty with cork-grains from their packings.

I went to school with children who had rags
for handkerchiefs pinned against loss
to their thin jerseys, who scuffed along
in clumsy boots too large for them,
whose clothes smelled dirty. I've since
learned for myself cleanness costs money.

Lord keep us safe this night we sang
at every school day's end, and once a year
came Empire Day – white clothes sashed
with the flag's colours; Rule Britannia,
Heart of Oak; the tented maypole patterns.

Fridays we danced Peasecods and Brighton Camp,
setting to partners in the hall beneath the eyes
of Sir Galahad and Jesus with a lantern,
framed in Pre-Raphaelite foliage.
We made our own pictures with waxy crayons,
satisfied with our suns – orange blobs
rayed round with stiff spider-legs – until
standing disgraced, face to the classroom wall,
we learned to reject such simplicity.

At iron-framed scarred desks we sat in pairs,
practised handwriting, loaded our memories
with the Mad Hatter's Tea Party and Robin Hood.
We could draw a Roman helmet, and divide
the sentences of our mother tongue
into pencilled columns. At tables-time,
a wheel of numbers chalked on the board,
our teacher's tapping pointer demanded
instant answers – I in a fervour of dread,
blank-minded around the sevens and eights.

Before us lay long division and the solving
of problems remote from our young lives –
the filling and emptying of water tanks,
the relative speed of trains.

These things were taught us but without effort
other knowledge grew – the gloss and grain of things:
worn-smooth benches, the herring-bone of parquet,
playground asphalt, mottled cloakroom floors,
white china washbowls, brass taps, iron coathooks,
swinging heavy doors of varnished wood and glass,
the chalky fingers of teachers, white dust falling
from the blackboard rubbed clean.

Walking home through a suburb growing from old fields
I'd find flowers in fallow building sites –
abandoned cabbage-plants in bloom and daisies.
I would rush past the gate by the elder tree.
We all knew a witch lived there.

In my tenth summer, wearing
a cut-down dress of paisley-patterned voile,
I discovered the curve of my spine; female.
I walked aware in the dinner-time hot sun,
past the Finchley Press and Bradshaw's drapery,
the Black Bess Café where only men went,
two sweetshops, the greengrocer's, the Salvation Army,
the bakery with green cakes shaped like frogs,
the Home and Colonial's black glass and gold,
Bevan's the butchers, and Wright's wide door –
sacks and bins on a wood floor, dried peas
ready-soaked to sell by the pint measure,
and yellow chicks in the shop window
struggling for place round a warm lamp.

Then the last corner, the dark top-shop
with its long mahogany counter; groceries,
Meux's ale. The side door for Sundays
was in our road. Leicester Road.
Number thirty-six was home.

# Emma

I saw my mother cry for the first time
when Emma died;
she sat on my bed weeping.
Dead. What was dead?
A no more; too much to understand.

Lucky to have had an Emma,
to have loved her, every inch
of her five feet tall,
known every wrinkle, all
the mumbles of her jaw,
white hair of head and chin,
the rolling walk
her short leg gave her.

She would carry things
in a slung pocket between petticoats
(she wore five, black sateen,
to keep out cold and heat
both in due season).

Undressing for bed we would perform
and pirouette for her and she would sing
old songs about Jim Crow for lullaby
and nod herself to sleep.

She'd take all day to clean the stair-rods,
two hours to wash the dishes,
hated to go home, staying long after dark.

A pensioner, she came daily
for a little wage, her meals,
a lot of life. Our semi was her palace,
we her princes. When my mother flagged
or seemed inadequate she'd say,
'There's cart horses, m'm, and there's carriage horses;
they're not meant to be the same.'
Who would not weep to lose
so staunch a comforter?

# China Dolls

Sit them up – their eyes
spring to attention,
sapphire or sometimes brown
beneath feather-vaned brows.

Laid supine, matt-pink lids lowered,
they fall to an immediate sleep
too calm for dreams.
Propped amongst cushions

they can never drift into a doze;
nor can they lie awake staring
at ceiling or sky,
or with an exchange of glances

receive a goodnight kiss.
Always at a certain tilt
the weight swings –
*klup!* Eclipse.

Softly flushed cheeks, curved mouths
with rice-grain teeth, flawless
cylindrical throats – all these,
though they might well

last a childhood out
could come to grief as suddenly
as any chinaware.
A tumble might crack wide a head,

expose its hollowness –
a pallid bowl, unglazed – and *klup!*
a mechanism of strut and wire,
the blob of the counterpoise.

Face-down, were they open-eyed?
No matter; roughness of carpet, blanket,
garden grass, may press against glass
and cause no pain.

## Crystal Set

Our storybooks showed coloured plates
of men in khaki, a dry battleground,
yellow explosions, distant ruined trees.
Crouching with bayonets, or poised
like discus throwers, bomb in hand,
they were all heroes and all willing,
culled from the pink-girdled globe.

I remember the small sounds
of one November day: a crisp leaf
skittered along; a milkman's horse
scraped at the granite kerb; deep sobs
came from a lady in black clothes.
I held my mother's hand, stood still.
Nobody walked, no cars went by.

Later, school age, my brother
was given a crystal set.
Earphones pressed close, we listened
to the guns and then the silence.
Two minutes listening without a sound.
And then the bugles and the poem
about not growing old.


## House of Marvels

The Browns were the first to have the light –
even in daytime they would gladly demonstrate
the firm click of brass switches,
the dangling bulbs' obedience; and the house
had other wonders – there was a wireless set,
a tall cabinet paned with amber glass.
Rooted as sea-anemones to an aquarium floor
the valves glowed nervously, like new souls.

At the Browns' house there were no children
but I'd cross the road to visit, see the wireless
and the back garden's immaculate oblong lawn,
the disciplined blaze of calceolarias, lobelia,
geraniums. Trowel, water-can and wheelbarrow
stood on the path, ready, speckless as new toys.

Even the cellar was admirable, the white
and black of it – wisely-bought coal exhaling
its tingling, mineral, odour all summer.
And then upstairs to wash hands. A white coverlet,
the bed flat as a tray, smooth as if unenjoyed.
Beyond imagining, his greying moustache,
her putty cheeks, against those shrouded,
bolstered pillows. On the bedside pot-cupboard
a half-full bottle, upturned tumbler.
Mrs Brown follows my gaze. 'Vichy,' she says.
'Special water…from a spring in France.'
Another marvel, surely. I think of the blue
stoneware mug my father takes upstairs
filled from the ordinary tap.


## Hungry Thirties


Under the streetlamp he'd shake off rain
from his stiff cape, blow on mittened hands.
In summer, the suburbs in bloom like villages,
he'd arrive hatless, thumb on the rasping bell,
shoe toeing the curb, cycle-clipped leg
taut as he stretched from the high saddle.
His old green machine, unskilfully repainted
cast-off from a Stop-me-and-buy-one fleet,
was loaded with books instead of snofrutes.

Our parents would stand in the narrow hall,
or on the tiled path warm-evening-free together.
His stock of forgotten novels, each re-covered
in brown wrapping-paper, must be considered
and discussed. His was a persuasive voice,
low, laced with a sloshy lisp.

'Mr Johnson' (offering a not-recent whodunnit)
'likes a good murder...' 'Mrs Johnson likes' –
here a sly glance – 'a bit of love.'
He would place in my mother's hand
a dog-eared bit of love.

A character, my father would say.
We knew his tone, part mockery, part respect;
knew that the weekly sub, small sop to fortune,
was tribute to that stringy, brave, old man
who could expect no Friday payday;
who, pedalling, talking, toting shabby books,
kept himself alive on tuppences.


## The Smell of Tar


From oblique conversations, the details
glossed over, I still understood
that someone like me, in round-toed shoes,
shouldering a satchel heavy
with books and rattling pencil-box,
who'd walked home in the winter dark
towards just such a tea-table as ours,
just such a fire-lit room, had met
with the terror they whispered of
had never reached her door.

Our roadway was of wood, a rough parquet
steeped in tar. The season of her death
the blocks were pickaxed out, piled up
in pungent stacks under the streetlamps
and along the unlighted stretches where, garden
to shallow garden, crouching shadows slipped –
clumsy, bearlike, silent; ready to be quick.
Something that stalked behind black privet,
lurked by porch and gate, had caught...
With all my life to live, I ran
to my heart's limit, gulping tarry air.

# Passing Away

When there was mortal sickness in a house
straw would be spread across the the road.
Cars would go slowly past. The daily horses
(muscular, bell-hooved, for hauling coal,
glossy and amiable, with doorstep milk)
trod through with muffled steps.

Nothing to see. Behind an upstair window
someone got on with their dying,
a drama far removed by purgative time
from life's beginnings in a wilder bed –
a sexless enactment this, deserving
smoothed sheets, quiet witnesses.

Sound waited on the event. Footfalls,
the grind of wheels, must not distract or hurt
the closing senses. The scene could only be
imagined – grey head against dinted pillow,
deepened eyes by turns supplicating and resigned,
and women in soft shoes, listening,

bending to hear the last faint words,
faint even in the sick-room's hush.
Below, the street held its breath, waiting
for the sign, patent as papal smoke, the rasp
of ring along rod, the curtain drawn across
by an unseen and careful hand.

# Birthday Party

*Poor Jenny is a-weeping...*

We circle hand in hand
passing the room's landmarks
sofa and chairs pushed back,
fireplace, door, window
with a glimpse of green –

*on a bright summer's day.*

small shape in the mosaic
that stretches ever-widening
towards the meadowlands
past Totteridge and Barnet.

*On the carpet she shall kneel*
*while the grass grows in the field.*

Head bowed, palms
pressed to tearless cheeks
she knows from the outset

*Stand up. Stand up on your feet*
*and choose the one...*

who'll be her best beloved;
knows we'll wish her joy.


# Two Stalls at the Bedford

The jokes were above my head
and the high-kicking chorus girls
in plumes and glittering costumes
seemed to me as pointlessly employed

as the pairs of comics loudly arguing
while laughter burst from stalls and gallery
and from the boxes, grandly lipped
and curved, crusted with mouldings.

Sickert's eye had rested there
gauging the glow on flesh and plaster
and, large as life, Belle Elmore
had her brief hour on the boards –

names unknown to me then; and I can't guess
what stars of vaudeville I may have seen
and not remembered – yet there's
recall of colour and of shadow:

the slide of crimson velvet, the stage
golden across half-darkness, high
long-reaching shafts of light and lazy
lifting swirls of grey-blue smoke.

After, a stone-floored passage,
red buckets, sand and fag-ends, and out
by the push-bar door into a shuffling
brick-walled alley. Yellow lamps,

Camden Town's cold pavements, the wait
for a bus. Headful of sound and colour.
Flushed skin shrinking from the wind.
A speechless ache for home and bed.

My mother's gaiety spilling down –
*Did you like it?.......Wasn't it good?*

*Belle Elmore was the stage-name of Mrs Crippen.*

# Remembering Menuhin

On my first day away from home
we walked in the park. The bare grey path
seemed to stretch endlessly. Slight trees
semaphored in a March wind that searched
my skirt with an icy tongue, found flesh
above stocking-tops.

My aunt lived upstairs – the upper floor
of a semi in Willesden Green. In the small
room where I slept the bed fitted tight
against three of its walls, a close
safe place, but I missed my mother.

Each hour was a slab of boredom.
Except one day as we ate roast lamb
and then rice pudding, and then drank tea
a violin played – all that time -
from the wireless. 'Imagine!' said my aunt,
'Only a boy, playing like that!'

And every morning there were the ten minutes
when we watched from our window,
across a convent wall. The older nuns
walked briskly, marching pairs;
the young ones within their long black skirts
dodged and pursued each other, playing tag.
They ran about on the grass between the paths
of the closed garden, almost dancing
though no music could be heard.

# Love Lyrics

He'd take it from the stiff
black leather box where it lived
safe on a high shelf. Razor;
dangerous elegant instrument,
his personal property and privilege.
It flashed as he stropped
skimming the dark supple strap.
We heard the soft thumping rhythm,
and the song. Tosti's Goodbye.
*You that I worshipped so.*

We'd loll in the bathroom doorway
while he lathered up, cut skilful
flat swathes through the marshmallow soap.
Still he sang, that young man who since
has had no choice but to grow old
and die. *Less than the dust,* he sang,
*Beneath thy chariot wheels.*

Brushing his red-gold hair he'd lean
towards the mirror and sing con espressione
*Pale hands I loved beside the Shalimar.*
We glimpsed worlds to come,
our own true loves.

I had not then heard, whispered
between the rows of damp school coats,
the facts of sex; had much more to learn.
His songs had not been for my mother alone,
a duplicity the years disclosed.
There was no more singing, no bright
old-fashioned blade. He took to the tame
safety razor, closed the bathroom door.

# Big Girl Next Door

*(for Glendora Barton,*
*died August 1994, in Tasmania)*


She's veiled and in satin,
I'm in ice-blue ring velvet –
slight then, and shivering
bare-armed on the steps
of All Saints' porch.

Oatmeal face-packs the evening before,
fighting down laughter. My hair
twisted up with curling tongs
falling limp and straight
within an hour.

She walked with such a swing
her clothes seemed fluid.
I remember a white dress,
square neck banded with red and blue
for the old king's jubilee.

Another, slinky brown satin, cowled
with coral at the neck. Clothes
enjoyed, and paid for week by week,
a tithe to the club man.
And how alive and lithe she was

in the bias-cut guinea gowns
I couldn't wait to achieve,
lumping around in serge gymslip,
a blazer that allowed for growth.
My swimsuit was regulation black –

she wore one of many colours,
back bare between the wings
of an entire butterfly handknitted
in three-ply wool – a work of art
that water would have ruined.

In her going-away suit of cossack cut,
her hat of mock astrakhan – brown,
like those velvet-brown eyes – she stays
secure in memory. I've no photographs
to age her, slow her stride.


## Then


The earth was dark and soft,
thinly grassed through a spattering
of sharp gravel. We stood in the arm
of a buttress, against All Saints'
night-browned red brick.

Fuzzed and diffused
as if by all Finchley's breath,
the streetlamps' yellow touched
faint highlights along the restless
bare limbs of pathside shrubs;

but neither light nor wind
reached where we sheltered.
Pressed close in thick coats
we'd kiss each other into a daze.
Restrained by risk as we were

who now would call us lovers?
We never lay down together
except in Hampstead's summer grass,
never embraced in a house
or naked or between sheets.

Yet our concord held
through a year's heat and cold.
Our long walks – to Muswell Hill
or down the Great North Road –
were one untiring conversation.

# The Exile

The summer over, we'd meet at the Odeon
or in a warm pub, with company.
Through all that year of ours he gave
little of himself, unless obliquely.
One night he borrowed his father's car,
drove us north, and without explanation
stopped in a pitch-dark lane, silently waited.

Suddenly – 'Here she comes!'
He pulled me by the hand, rushed me along.
A humpbacked bridge, brickwalled,
a pulse, a distant pinpoint of vermilion,
the low shine of railway lines.

A growing nimbus raced the long stretch
towards us, red-stained the wintry mist.
The unison of track, wheels, steam,
rose to crescendo. Sound and fire
leapt to embrace the arch.
The blaze of the hearth, the long line
of lit carriages, plunged through.

He said I'd remember, and I do, the Flying Scot
burning its way the length of England,
great pistons striving, cloud-white vapours
streaming back, darkness and silence
healing after.
                    But he, I think, was never
whole, looking always towards Scotland.
I wonder, did he take the other London girl,
the one he married, to wait on the dark bridge,
witness the night train...

# Heart or Head

Once in a suburban street he pulled sprays
of lilac from someone else's hedge
and decked me with it, bunched it round
like a sumptuous boa, becoming
as the silver fox the filmstars wore.

That was broad daylight, a lustrous evening.
Next winter he proposed romantically
on Waterloo Bridge, as we leaned on the parapet
in a secret interval between the high lamps
that bled flower-yellow light into the fog.

Meeting now, after many years, we don't
speak of lilacs or the November river.
Our lives have moved diametrically apart
(as he, young Marxist, primed with the formulae,
might have said). Much as we used to do

we share easy conversation, laughter.
He's well-married, published, travelled,
citizen of a university and of the world.
The aura of success, that powerful aphrodisiac,
moves me, at last and too late, to fancy him.

# Burnham Overy Staithe

## 1

My fourth summer; I'm sitting on a donkey
by a cottage gate.

From that first holiday I remember much.
Dark parlour furniture; the planked back door
where one day a huge fresh-caught skate
hung from a nail; the seashore at low tide,
shining, without a footprint; grey salt-grass;
the clear east-coast light.

I remember the front-garden path,
and the fence where the donkey stood
but of the donkey, now faint in sepia,
I have no recall.

## 2

They hear the bump of my fall, my cry,
come running to lift me from the cold floor
bringing the lamp's glazed and timid flame.
White walls in out-of-square perspective
soar towards a distant, shadowy, ceiling.

Summer, eyes culling like bees, thought-cells
ready to distil the essences garnered
on this long absence from the sameness
of pavement walks; from the house
that held me close as in a shell.
There, all familiar; here, all new –
the waves tumbling through hoops of light,
lipping the beach, clawing back, leaving
a scatter of pink fingernails to mark
the bubbled edge the sand drank up.

### 3

My chin rests on the rim of the rowboat,
a curved ledge of wind-bitten wood.
My dipping hand trails its own small wake.

Out from the shore the rowing stops;
the black-and-white bitch and her litter of five
are put over the side. The boat is turned for home.
Rippling folds flow back from the push
of each desperate puppy's breast.
Black berry-snouts tilt up for breath.
Legs beat like new-wound clockwork.

The boat is beached. Like moles into daylight
they struggle from the waves. Their mother
shakes showers from her coat, runs about,
receives the fishermen's praise.
I stand among the booted legs,
wrung with relief and joy.

### 4

The tide searched forward in shallow curves,
drained back fast to the waves' tumble,
to gather and reach again, and further.
It filled castle moats, dissolved turrets,
cast up a border of shells and weed and then
rushed thievishly off – my tin pail,
with its primary-bright boys and girls,
starfish and crabs and pebbles,
bobbing away too fast for rescue.

My father and I, out in the early morning,
caught sight of a blue and yellow arc
lodged between sand-ripples. Our delving fingers
brought out the rest, my bucket, good as new.
The sea had held it gently, brought it back.
Rinsed and dried, it was allowed to stand
on that day's breakfast table, more treasured
for the moment than my silvered knife,
my china cup – *A Present for a Good Child.*

**5**

I should have looked at the map first,
been forewarned that the limitless sea
I saw with my small-child's eyes
is a sludgy landlocked channel –
tidal, yes; the sea did take my pail.

I'm not alone, there's not much time
and anyway this, now, is a tourist place.
I don't look for the cottage – but, leaving,
I see something I surely recognise.
A heavy baulk, thick as a man's waist,

silvered from salt and weather, scarred,
bearded with weed and bladderwrack,
rooted, for who knows what outdated purpose,
in the bank's khaki mud. Its actuality
still can't quite oust my saffron sands.


## Legs


Chill early sunlight, high hedges,
the glitter of beaded spider webs.
He holds my hand; my hurrying's
a rill beside his steady river.

A gate plushed with moss; the magic
meadow. I dance amongst night-set
constellations, run, dart, twirl,
rush weightless across the grass.

The mushrooms are not gathered,
not taken home – the memory's
momentary; there's no conclusion.
But, if only for an instant,

my young legs spring to life –
spontaneous, elastic, agile,
a glimpse of something I once knew:
how a child skips along, how a lamb leaps.

## Dallinghoo

Long summers spent
in rich fields
cloth of buttercup gold
in rickyards
idling on the loose stacks
lungs full of musty straw-fume

C'mon chicks! at that cry
I'd run too
help to scatter the grit-hard
cool grains of maize
casting from side to side
a slow comet orbit of the yard
dragging a turbulent tail

Then the search for eggs
for the secret places
where the hens would lay
beneath old axles
in holes in the hay
under the hens themselves
who'd squawk and fuss and flap off
when we surprised them

Rust-feathered wings clipped
they couldn't rise far
couldn't sail over the fences
where they might raise their young
if there were food enough there
and no foxes

# Harvest

They were summers full of sunshine. In the fields
we would creep into the stooks of tilted sheaves,
crouching with scratched legs
among the sharp-cut stubble. Tight to dry earth
too low for blades to catch grew speedwell
blue as cornflower, pimpernel
red as poppy.

From two-tined shining forks, long handles worn
to patina by hard palms, the sheaves flew high
onto carts lead-red and blue-sky painted.
The wheels rolled heavy-hubbed and iron-rimmed
weightily field to stack and lighter back again
between straw-littered hedges dull with dust.

As the day drooped to evening we'd ride the wide backs
of Boxer or Diamond to the farmyard. Freed from shafts,
greasy black straps swinging, they could wade
into the pond, drink, bend their great necks.
It was the men's joke not to lift us down
but thwack the chestnut rumps, send us to balance
above the surface smeared with sap-green weed.

They teased us, town children, made us brave;
and I remember them, the faces, names, speech,
working clothes and movements of those men,
the perks they carried home; skimmed milk in cans,
field cabbages in sacks, soft rabbits
swinging head-down from loops of twine, to feed
long families of uncombed dusty children
who stood at laneside gates,
watched us without a smile.

# Mille Fleurs

Étoile d'Hollande was to come later –
deep crimson. The old roses never glowed
with such dark richness. In the cottage garden
most were pinkish red – climbing Alexandra, single
and golden-stamened; cabbage-roses along the wall,
saucer-heads crammed with petals; moss roses
struggling through veils of feathery cosmos,
love-in-a-mist, night-scented stock.

For grown-ups' birthdays we'd buy Woolworth perfumes –
Jasmine, Mille Fleurs, or Jockey Club. Sixpence
seemed dear for such a tiny flask, while in the garden
scent was everywhere – and free.
So, rain thrumming all day on the tarry shed's old roof,
we crushed and pounded roses, steeped the pulp
in water, were surprised when the strained essences
ran brown, gave out faint smells of rot.

The recipients' delight, we knew, was feigned;
but we kept trying through that stormy August,
tried with honeysuckle, pinks, sweet peas
and with the soft mauve cottony heads
of mint in bloom, encouraged in such a quiet,
contained pursuit – until the sun shone again,
and we could roam the meadows.

## By the Fuchsia
*(for John Manning)*

Each summer we forgot high ceilings, switched-on light,
full taps, took easily to oil lamps, primuses, the preciousness
of water. Our earth closet was along the path; a wooden bench,
a sprinkler tin of disinfectant powder. Thick-grown ivy
made a tunnel to next-door's privy – Johnnie's.

It was Johnnie who worked both the gardens, brought vegetables
to August ripeness, and sometimes let us for a while into his
room, his parlour, haunted with smells of hard block soap and age
and abstinence. The floor was coral brick, mottled and worn.
A dark rug of hooked rags lay by the hearth, two china dogs
stared from the mantelpiece. The grate was his only heat.
Each morning he'd chop faggots for his kindling, coax
the cradled twigs to flame, get the sooted kettle singing.
Midday, he'd set his meal, newspaper spread on the deal table:
white bread, strong cheese, raw onion. He pared off slices,
carried them to his mouth steadied against his thumb on the moist
blade of the pocket-knife he used to cut twine, whittle sticks.
Once a week the bread was new; by the seventh day he ate it
mouldy, staled to hardness. He had no cushion, no soft seat.
Two wooden chairs stood by the white wall and a flour-hutch,
massive, oaken, empty. A pair of stuffed snipe in a glass case
prompted his tales of poaching and gamekeeping –
he'd done both, told tricks of how to hide, how find.
His beard was kept in an old country style – a white ruff
for a shaven face. His speedwell eyes had never seen a city.

Old, alone, poor almost as the poorest, he never seemed other
than content, relishing what he had – few possessions,
simplest food, sun, fireside, sometimes beer or baccy;
no entertainment but a wind-up gramophone, one hymn.
*Abide with Me.* When, in his seventies, he died, his dog
ran to its death beneath the wheels of the hearse.
The next summer I thought I saw Johnnie at his door, bent
to one side as always, the huge-soled boot on his short leg
resting on the step. And so I see him still, by the fuchsia,
his gaze direct and gentle, as when I knew him
a long time ago, when I was a child.

# Veteran

He was taught by the local builder, who also
made coffins and sold petrol – R O P
from a long-necked pump – a strong, stout man.
They'd sit high and breezy in his Model T Ford,
change places without getting out, heaving
up and under along the black bench-seat.
A few miles along narrow stone-strewn lanes
and he'd become a driver.

In that quiet country cars could still surprise.
Ponies reared in the shafts of traps, hens flapped
in clumsy panic to the hedge as he drove by, elbow
on the klaxon button, tyres whirling up dust.
Sometimes there'd be a steam-roller spreading
a first coat of tar, but as yet few fellow-motorists,
unless on a day at the coast – Southwold or Felixstowe,
or shopping at Wickham Market – the butcher's first
with its wooden block and latticed shutters,
a few yards on from the AA's yellow plaque
that war would confiscate, and the laneside sign:

Speed Limit
10 mph.

# Passing Marks Tey

I used to see the old men sunning themselves,
a village parliament by the south side of a barn.
Grass clumped by the wall; between the uprights
of the bench the earth was bootworn, brown.

I could almost smell the ashy bowls of the pipes
they sucked, their musty hats, as we passed through
towards deeper country where men in the fields
straightened their backs when motorcars went by.

36

We travelled into Suffolk, slowed by punctures
and running-board picnics. My father's bargain tourer
had a toolbox, a starting handle, a leather hood.
Such cars belong to the rich now, or to museums.

When I drove through Essex I passed Marks Tey
on a fast road; saw no bench, no new old men.
I thought of them indoors watching faces that can't listen
and plays about peace and war impeccably researched.


## Innocence


He took to the ocean in a costume
of surely Edwardian origin –
loose, with tubular legs,
of a thin black cotton.

His stroke was the trudgeon – he also
swam on his back, circling an old hull,
kicking up white spray against its shadow
and waving to prove his pleasure.

Then out, and gingerly across
the shelving shingle beach
to stand before us, shedding rivulets,
shivering a little.

Wet cloth clung to chest, ribs, navel;
and moulded, close as cling-film,
to the curious coquillage embossed
at the meeting of his thighs.

My mother and the mistress, rummaging
in their beachbags, vied
to hand him towels, hot coffee,
sandwiches, a chocolate bar.

# Romany Blood

Steam turned the roundabouts,
powered coloured lights, made the music.
Men rode the rides, re-set coconuts,
loaded air-guns, held out stained hands
for coppers. Their pockets sagged,
they wore no collars.

*My grandmother was a Lee –*
Thus he'd introduce himself to travellers,
fairground people, eagerly dragging us
by the hand into a town square transformed.
Reflective smoke clouds roofed it in;
its walls were noise.

We were small and shy; he found us a friend,
a ten-year-old, confident from summers
on the road, her own bank of swingboats.
She let us swing and swing, gaudy chenille
running soft through our palms. When at last
we'd had enough the lifted brake-bar
scraped beneath us, brought us to the wooden step.

My great-grandmother was a Lee; the blood's
thinner now. Only my brother has the Romany
eyes and skin, the trading instinct. My father
had a Saxon look, with his blue eyes. I see
that they were courteous to him, but at base
indifferent, those close-knit secret people.

# The Half-Mile

I was twelve when I swam the half-mile,
up and down the tide-fed cold concrete
pool, with a slow steady sidestroke.
My father counted the lengths,
at first from the deep-end board
and then, as I moved more laboriously,
pacing alongside, urging me on.

The race was only against myself
and distance. The grainy salt water,
though not translucent like the chlorinated
blue lidos of town, buoyed me helpfully,
lapped softly against the bath's grey sides
variegated with embedded hardcore pebbles.
I swam from goal to alternate goal; he counted.

When he called enough I scrambled
over the sharp shutter-cast lip,
shuddered into a dry towel, drank
the words of praise. The planks
of the changing-room walls
were warm to touch. It had seemed to be
a great deal of swimming; still does.


# Mrs Blake

She'd push into the waist-high jumble of her garden, fingers
sliding the stems to cradle calices, draw single flowers near,
familiar with each shape and scent, each lineage.

With four tall goats she rambled the lanes year-round,
talked to them while, avid and angular, they reared
against hedgerows, champed the topmost shoots.

Trudging along, in torn overcoat, rough boots,
white hair wisped in the wind, she looked
like a needy countrywoman; was, the village said, a lady.

Her voice was evidence, and her courtesy. She invited me,
a diffident adolescent, for morning coffee.
We sat in a square of lawn spared from the rampant foliage.

She set out well-used fine porcelain. I watched
her weathered face, the kind lines, serene blue eyes,
and the earthgrained hands tilting the silver pot.

Apart by more than fifty years, we liked each other.
At evening she'd put on soft shoes, move quietly
about the house, her hard and fissured hands

gentle around cups and cupboards. We'd sit together
in the summer dusk, she on the windowseat
in faded dress, hair puffed round a velvet ribbon.

The room smelled of damp wainscots, crumbling books,
lamp oil, wood ash – she had no unwavering light,
no water tap; flame and the rain sufficed.

Married beneath her. It was said as if her lacks
were somehow punishment for breaching rules;
for choosing, decades ago, the life she wanted.


# Wood


Stands of deal, pitchpine and beech
came through the workshop door, went out
reshaped. For years, against the far wall
a stack of wide planks leaned untouched.
My coffin-wood, he'd say. No hurry.

Easy to speak of coffins when blood's warm,
when the plane slides surely, the saw,
shedding pale pyramids of mealy dust,
bites without effort through the grain
crafting doors, cupboards, window-frames –
and coffins fit for all the parish.
But not the large box needed
for his bull-strong big-bellied girth.

Plenty of time…but the hand slows,
hard muscle softens, time contracts.
His last rest, after all,
was in an undertaker's town-made box,
its gloss sprayed on. His way had been
to buff the smoothed wood with hard wax,
sweat to perfect the lustre, even though
for so few hours it would last unspoiled.


## Light


It must have been harvest moon –
the night air warm, the lane
breathless,
smoothed.
At the grassy triangle
where three lanes come together
stood the man, whose body
I don't forget
though there was never
a touch between us;
though he was hale and old
and I not long
past childhood.

Iron-grey curling hair.
Shirt loose on his chest.
Strong legs a little bowed.
A touch of the faun.

Under the huge moon
drenched in light
drinking light
he waited.

Each moon
a once-only.
I saw the man
still as a tree.

*Where have you been?* they said
ready for bed
waiting up.
I knew I'd come home
with a mystical face
rapt, satisfied.
*You've been so long...*


## Wattle and Daub


*Best water for brewing ale*
the old man would say,
drawing up murky bucketfuls
from the pond behind the back'us.

The other pool was cupped in steeper banks,
grown round with bramble, campion,
woody nightshade. A shaky ladder
dipped through mosaics of duckweed
to where languid mottled carp
swam and multiplied.

The land had no well, no spring;
we valued every drop that rushed
down the pantiles' curves in summer storms,
gurgled through gutter and downpipe
into the tall tarred barrel.

Red wormlets and minute transparent larvae
writhed in the water dippered out
for all our washing.

Those before us had taken rain from pond
and water-butt for every need.
We, town-bred, would drive to a neighbour farm,
hump home lidded churns of pump-water
that poured clear for drinking.

First came an outdoor standpipe.
Later, water gushed into porcelain,
swept away privy, zinc bath, chamber pot.
The ponds, hollowed four centuries back
to yield the cottage clay, are quenched now,
levelled, little arboured lawns
for shady sitting-out on summer days.


## Yellow Kite
*(Walberswick)*


Fine white strings run taut
across October's Sunday blue,
barely visible stays
from hand to kite.

A man teases the wind,
standing on tussocky grass,
eyes fixed on the shining shape
he draws across the sky.

He dances it, loop upon loop,
wide circles, figures of eight.
Captive, it bobs and tugs; red tail
coils and uncoils in its wake.

The father's intent, absorbed.
The child looks down,
makes patterns in the sand
with shells, with pebbles.

# Mabel Winifred Christina

She gave birth to me on their feather bed
with its high mahogany head and foot, figured
and finialled. Between pitchpine struts
the chain-mail spring sagged like a sailor's hammock.

The bedroom was lilac and mimosa –
favoured colours then. On the dressing-table
a flowered china trinket-set not for touching
held rings, brooches, a lidded gold watch
enamelled with geisha girls.
The ottoman had its mauve loose cover,
the window nets their brass rods.

Within the welter of walls, floors, furniture,
comforts and satisfactions, she was the central
presence – composed or hurried, excited, laughing,
angry; at times in pain, uncertain or afraid.
I'd find myself contented or perplexed,
the womb still a subliminal encirclement.

In early years the mother's too close a being
for the child to see. My glimpses of her are few
and nebulous. Definition came, I think,
with my puberty – and then she seemed past youth.

## Semi-detached

The tap marked hot in the bathroom
was dry; for a bowlful
of hot water, kettles must be boiled,
carried upstairs. Easier,
the morning chores done,
for my mother to fill an enamel
basin, wash herself at the kitchen table.

She would screw tight
her marmalade hair, take off
her glasses and blouse, stand
in her shiny slip. The heat
flushed her fair skin,
almost raised weals
on her neck. Her eyes seemed wary;
an angry score of red linked them
across the bridge of her nose.
Pearly water dripped
from her elbows, ran down
between her breasts. I was glad
when a hasty towelling and a clean blouse
brought her back to me unchanged.

## Doorsteps

Cutting bread brings her hands back to me –
the left, with its thick wedding-ring,
steadying the loaf. Small plump hands
before age shirred and speckled them.

She would slice not downwards but across
with an unserrated ivory-handled carving knife
bought from a shop in the Edgware Road,
an Aladdin's cave of cast-offs from good houses –
earls and countesses were hinted at.

She used it to pare to an elegant thinness.
First she smoothed already-softened butter
on the upturned face of the loaf. Always white,
Coburg shape. Finely rimmed with crust the soft
halfmoon half-slices came to the tea table
herringboned across a doylied plate.

I saw away at stoneground wholemeal.
Each slice falling forward into the crumbs,
to be spread with butter's counterfeit,
is as thick as three of hers. Doorsteps,
she'd have called them. And those were white
in our street, rubbed with hearthstone
so that they glared in the sun
like new-dried tennis shoes.


## Grandparents


I've only one memory of him.
The viewpoint's level with the tucked-in
counterpane of a high hospital bed.
He sits upright against pillows in a full
wide-striped nightshirt, his beard
awesomely black against white linen,
white-painted iron bed, speaking
to the grown-ups, not to me.

Tales of his eccentricities
are all I came to know of him.
My grandmother, it was said,
had not dared to lift her eyes in chapel
lest they chanced to meet those of a man.
Upon her he wrought thirteen babies.

I, child of the thirteenth,
neglected to ask my mother –
had she loved him? Had he ever been
tender towards her – ever generous?

She would speak sometimes
of her mother's gentleness,
the silk patchwork she sewed
in moments of rest.


## Tuesdays


My great-aunt visited each Tuesday,
wearing a highblocked brown straw hat
swathed with brown pleated satin.
A fine-meshed veil was stretched
from brim to beneath her chin.
My kiss met a honeycomb of threads.

Nappa gloves cased her fingers,
her narrow nails; filbert, she used to say.
Her suit, brown serge, was tailored
to a pattern chic in nineteen-ten,
coat well past the hips, long skirt,
satin-stitched arrowheads.

Indoors, the several long knobbed pins
drawn out, she'd loose the veil,
lift up the hat with both hands
by the crown, stab it again with pins.
Carefully set on the hall table
it waited her departure.

I recall no other clothes of hers,
except... (eyes dark beyond smiling;
a straggle of hair across the pillow)
long-laundered pin-tucked cotton,
buttoned cuffs... a white nightgown.

## C.A.N.C.E.R.

Admiring the bygones our grandmothers
remember in daily use, we shop
for lamps, workboxes, polished kettles,
and the thick plush table-covers
that in proper households kept dark
the gloss of parlour mahogany.

My great-aunt's out-of-fashion clothes
disguised for many months
the wasting of her substance.
Grey-faced, admitting at most
to a twinge of indigestion,
she preserved her body's privacy
beyond any hope of help.

Imparting shocking news, her way
had been to whisper above our heads.
'Imagine! Poor soul – D.E.A.D. by morning...
B.L.double-O.D. all over...'
No spelling out her own distress.
In the house of her childhood
piano legs had worn skirts
and nothing been seen naked
that decent cloth might dress.

## Casualties

There was dust on her sideboard
and she had a lodger, lugubrious man
who carried tea to her in bed.
We were taught to think her frivolous

or worse. Instead of dusting she'd sit
in the garden and read Mary Webb
while the lodger pottered, planted.
He was less than consort to her queen,

she made that clear, no consolation
for the young husband, foundered
in anonymous mud at Passchendaele,
two weeks out of England and newly-wed.

The baby, grief's frail doll,
had died on a pillow in her arms.
Of small concern thereafter how thick
the dust, who brings the morning tea.


## My Mother Loved to Flirt


There was the master-butcher, Charles, who brought
gifts of his special sausages, prime pork.
I liked his looks; he had a widow's peak,
his strong black hair was Brylcreemed to a gloss.
He'd stay an hour or so; they'd laugh and talk.

And then, how good the tea-time fry-up tasted!
My father, always one to relish fat,
would clean his plate, exclaiming
'Good old Charlie,' and 'Money can't
buy better food than that.'

# The Romantic

A Goldsmith's man, an Arts and Crafts schoolmaster,
he'd turn his hand to landscapes, forms in plaster,
repoussé work. One spring (he liked things shipshape)
he gave our dining-room a mural seascape –
a painted fleet of galleons under sail.

He cut innumerable stencils, and we children
abandoning the joys of street and garden
were under orders – *Dab* it on. Don't brush it!
And *evenly!*... We weren't supposed to rush it –
blurred outlines and the whole affair might fail.

There were stencils for the hulls, for crested billows,
for pennants, buoys, seabirds, sails plumped like pillows
and single summer clouds. One then another
we overlaid the cut-outs, shaded colour.
A thousand shapes all came together pat

and there above the dado was the crowning
of all our hours stepladder up-and-downing,
stiff necks and fingers' blue, red, yellow staining
and being indoors when the sun was shining –
the towering Tudor men-o'-war complete,

blazoned with cross and fleur-de-lys and eagle.
He wasn't very good at drawing people
so none appeared on castle-deck and galley.
His tall ships rode as if by magic spell. He
set no mariner on shroud or spar
and left unmanned the crow's-nest and the oar.

# The Mistress

She put away her hats,
the deep-crowned felts and straws
that had housed her bun of hair.
Marcelled and shingled
she seemed to shed spinsterhood
almost be made anew.

At first it had been a cushioned lap,
a hand I reached up to hold,
the angle of familiar feet –
strap shoes with louis heels.
I knew her busy step, opaque stockings,
plain serge skirts. And then one Christmas
a dress of dove-grey marocain,
low-sashed; a long necklace,
dangling, tasselled. She smelled
of lavender and vanishing cream.

Once, I believe, I glimpsed her naked
through a half-open door.

Partisan daughter, I learned to resent
the auntish gifts that had bribed my childhood
so easily – sweets, stamps, pennies;
began to see how sycophancy worked
on a vain man's heart; knew why
my mother would sometimes shrug away
my father's hand, would flinch
from a compliment as from a sting.

# Ice

*Coffee?* she'd say brightly, getting up
from her fireside seat – and I'd have no choice
but to follow her out of the warmth
into that freezing kitchen.

Waiting for the kettle, we'd set out
biscuits and glacial china on a tray.
To fight the shivers I'd fold my arms,
hands tucked into armpits.

But I had to stay, helping; after all
it was my fiancé sitting back there
beside my vacated cushion on the sofa,
listening to our wireless as usual

and ready to make a fourth at solo.
Seemingly amicable, all evening
she'd loose sly barbs against him.
They riled me, fed my obstinacy.

Two winters passed before I gave back
that three-stone diamond ring.


# Looking North

He was a South-of-Watford man.
Few places that lay North of that marker
gained his approval – though parts of Suffolk
were O.K., and he tolerated Wales, especially
the area around Llandrindod Wells.

As far as he was concerned Northampton,
Durham and Derby scarcely existed.
It's taken me a lifetime to revise his judgements –
to discover, for instance, that Manchester
is no wetter than Cornwall, and has theatres,

even a tree or two. Liverpool especially
came as a surprise, my having been brought up
to believe it a city in which no sensible person
would wish to set foot, let alone settle.
An aunt who went to live there

was spoken of almost as if dead.
He envisaged a pall of yellowish fog,
a population scarcely human – the dregs
of the world's most noisome seaports.
Of course he never went there

but I remember how his lip would curl
at the mere mention of Liverpool.


## Iced Coffee


They never afforded close carpeting,
only practical squares of brown
leaf-patterned Axminster, never
a washing-machine or a fridge.
It was always either one thing
or another, a balancing of choices.

One winter Sunday afternoon
my father sprang up suddenly
from the quiet of his chair, tugged
at his trouser pocket
and flung onto the hearthrug
a clattering handful of loose change
crying, 'That's what I am, a penny man!'

He longed for flamboyance –
a dashing Edwardian role,
tossing careless sovereigns.

Retirement freed him from the suburbs.
The dark-beamed rose-hung house
lent him at last the aura
of a leisured man of means.
He accepted village chairmanships,
kept geese and a bulldog, trundled
to Taunton in his old Humber, buying
buckets and fertilisers; would harvest
armfuls of vegetables, dump them
on the kitchen table, leave trails
of boot-mud on the terracotta shine –
all with an air of release, and pride
in everything from the mended thatch
to the new fridge against the larder wall.

On my first visit he settled me
in a garden chair, brought tall glasses.
His blue-eyed smile of triumph belied
his Noel Coward pose.
'Iced coffee?' he offered, casually.

## Last Visit

Bill Johnson is dead.
Almost I had forgotten
that the scared old man
shrunk in hospital bed,
whom I fed gently with a spoon,
once had been he. My father.
He had dwindled away, and no one
would countenance his fear.

I'm grateful I did not cheat him
with soft dishonesty
but found the needed words:
*Most of us are afraid.*

Then came a shadowless hour.
We talked like friends,
my hand in his frail hand
until, mid-thought, his voice
trailed into silence,
his lids drooped down, he slept.
I walked quietly down the ward,
paused at the door, looked back
as if to check on a child
settled for the night.

# Arm in Arm

I felt her softness within the loose
lopsided dressing-gown, the light bone
in the sleeve against my side. Her smile
was not whole nor her eyes steady –
she so wanted the un-aged girl in her
to live, however cruelly the years
had stripped her, breast and womb,
worn her with decades of coughing.

Peopled with friends, the hospital was for her
like college where more than sixty years before
she'd been the popular one, not least because
my father had once dared to come courting,
his arrival watched incredulously
from dormitory windows, while female dragons
got up steam for reprimand – righteousness
perhaps tinged with envy.

When she died I found their portraits:
his in artist's smock beside an easel,
hers summer-dressed, composed in studio sepia –
a young woman I never could have known,
whose life I was to change.
Remembering, I regret a moment of impatience.

We were pacing the long passage arm in arm
when she stopped, reached out a hand to waylay
a hurrying nurse, proudly presented me –
'My little daughter, come to visit.'
Appraising my size, my middle-age,
the nurse managed a forbearing smile
and rustled away with scarcely a pause.
We strolled on down the heartless corridor.

# 2 WAR

# Once upon a Time

War began on a Sunday
and the September sun shone,
shone on day after day
and I had nothing to do,
no plans;
lay idle in a hammock
slung between plum trees
eating their wealth
of fruit.

Through comfortable air
light and leaf-shadow
patterned me.
I don't remember any dark
only the ripe garden
and the warmth
and my life suspended
like the hammock swinging
waiting quietly
for the end of summer.


# A Victorian Painter
*(for Maud Angell)*

The calm of those late-summer days
trembled around us; a thin-skinned bubble –
who knew what might be in store?
Well over eighty, anxious to do her share,
she joined the line of neighbours
scooping sand into oblong sacks.

Soon we'd be bedding down in earthy shelters,
starting from sleep under tables and pianos
as the ack-ack guns let fly. A rain
of metal forged to bizarre arrowheads
would strike down, random, lethal.

Ruins would yawn mid-terrace.
Soon, but not yet.
September held us in its amber.
Plums fell golden from unruffled branches.

Miss Angell, amongst sofas, footstools,
cabinets of old porcelain and Wedgwood,
pale cameos on blue, soft green, basalt,
poured tea, talked of her travels.
Europe by train, with boxes, brushes, easel.
Portraits of gardens – rosewalks, vistas,
sumptuous borders – all commissioned.
And for decades of R.A. Summer shows
she'd painted flowers, massed in pitchers,
green glazed bowls, art-pottery jars.

Now she embroidered them, woolwork
improvised across coarse linen.
We drank from leaf-thin cups –
she wondering would she ever again
visit friends in Germany, in Dresden.
Already, women scarved for their tasks
were learning to drive rivets, weld,
solder, fold silken parachutes,
fill the bombers' armoury.


## War Damage, London N12


I'd thought of him as Mr Pinstripe –
quickmarcher to the morning bus,
well-shaven and glossy-collared,
the least likely of men to appear
immodestly in public.

He was in the bath when the bomb
sliced the house in two. He dropped
through dark confusion capsuled
in cast iron, was beached
on the piled ruins of his dining-room,

whole, but naked except for a pelt
of brick-and-mortar dust glued
to his wet skin with the blood
of his abrasions. Rumour said
it took five hours to make him clean.

Months later between the bathroom's
halved lino and the buried patterns
of the groundfloor carpet his dressing-gown
still sagged from a jutting nail
for any wind to tease.


## Wellington Pilot


One night I squirmed out
through the Waaf-site hedge
and for an hour or two
we lay in a dark strawstack
on the edge of a field;
cold East Yorkshire.

He told me that flying back
across the Kentish coast
he'd dip low over Folkestone.
His mother, awake before dawn,
would know it was B-Baker;
safe as yet.

A college boy, fair-haired,
prankish to hold off fate.
I'd watch the ops board
for his name.
A night erased him –
sweep of the duster,
soft fall of chalk.

# Bridlington

We'd take the train from the halt
not far from the camp's perimeter –
Arram to Brid. for the best
fish and chips we'd ever tasted,
a night out in illicit civvies.

Barbed wire hooped its way
along the land-side of the shore.
A string of dead lamps swung
in the sea-wind. The pier ballroom
corralled the light.

*In the Mood. Jealousy. Kalamazoo.*
We quickstepped, tangoed, waltzed
clasped to perspiring blue or khaki
almost always without conversation.
Except for the Czech soldiers.

Scrubbed faces, strangely folded caps;
stiff military manners. They stood
together, a small group, conferring
and then singly making the approach.
A bow. *You dance?* One or two circuits.

Then – *You sleep with me?*
We could feel corset bones beneath
the tailored uniforms, smell scent.
They didn't seem discouraged
when we shook our heads.

## Anorexia 1943

From skirt hem to the starched collar
loose on her starveling throat
was a mystery she preserved
through months of our close living.

We saw calves hardly walnut-sized
within the slack of her stockings
but somehow even in those clump-soled
RAF-issue lace-ups she was light-footed

busying about on spindle legs
that gave hint of the body I glimpsed
just once – gaunt armature of ribcage,
sternum, collarbones, nudging the skin.

Yet she could match us for stamina,
was cheerful, quick-minded,
immaculately pressed and polished.
She'd pretend to have eaten – we knew,

and hardly questioned, that she existed
on a sip or two of milk while we
rushed off to the mess for three square meals.
Never part of our evenings out, the wings

and rings and stripes and decibels
of Betty's Bar on a stand-down night,
she kept a shield of privacy,
and we ceased to invite.

Wiped away, the Nissen hut, the two rows
of iron beds. A score of faces forgotten
but not hers – great grey eyes, downy cheeks.
There was a faint sweetish smell on her breath.

We had no word then for what possessed her.

## Praying Hands

*(Albrecht Dürer – Albertina Library, Vienna)*

The postcard is scarred at each corner –
clusters of holes where thumb-tacks fastened it
to a succession of billet walls or to the beams
of Nissen huts, wherever we were housed.

The beds were always narrow, hard, weighed down
by stiff grey blankets. Young, we slept deeply
but we'd spring awake at the first sound
of the squadron's homeward beat, lie silent,

counting them in. We pretended then that death
was a light thing; the aircrews bought it,
went for a Burton, fell into the drink.
We looked for charms and icons; this was mine.

The hands are workmanlike; the nails pared close,
a fissure in one quick, capable curved thumb,
a spire of lightly-touching fingers – and as well
an unknown something, a perpetual question.

Yet surely in these hands the man's implicit,
a man five centuries entombed, who fasted, chanted,
tilled the earth; whose God lived changelessly
beyond the sky, and hurled no thunderbolts.


## Daphne Morse

I'd not thought of her for twenty years
except from time to time, coming across
the old snap of us at Scarborough,
its yellowed monochrome
showing us both laughing on the beach,
my springing red hair printed as dark
as her lustrous black.

Daphne Morse. We were always laughing together,
seeing façades as faces, windows as eyes,
sharing jokes and confidences.
And how we admired each other! And sought
adventure, making aimless journeys,
lodging in attics and cottages, discovering
high moors in the short summer.

It was so long ago, her death,
the scar of it healed, faded;
and yet today unreasonably, unprompted,
I've grieved with a clear bitterness
for her, shortlived
and lovely Daphne Morse.
Thought how her cheeks bloomed
and her throat was smooth
and so were mine, bloomy, smooth.

The looking-glass
is half my present grief.


## Manchester


A soiled light
faltered through the window,
died in the narrow room.
You lay like Eros on the shadowed bed.
I dared not look,
wanted no sight to read your darkness
nor any thought of time before or after
but a free-fall through the night.
These were the hours that could be
our last together.

The hotel
was half-destroyed by bombs,
gritty with brickdust
and everywhere abraded by hard years;
nap rubbed from the carpets,
life eroded out of the old men waiters,
the wallpaper sad fawn and blackened gilt,
chandeliers ready to fall
from their weight of dust.
We alone were young.

Two days we had.
Your train went north, mine
towards York across the Pennines.
Never before had the hills
seemed so green; in every valley
the sheltered mills shone
bright with illusory gold.

## The Cheval Glass

I saw how firmly we stood, breast
to breast – and we had longed for this;
white-pillowed bed, closed door,
the first secure embrace.

Yet while reflection held
my gaze – enraptured, sure –
came a mute peal of words:
What am I doing here?

As if he'd heard, he reached
to draw the curtains close,
make night of afternoon
and blind the looking-glass.

## Halifax Over 'Heartsease'

We came down low across the garden.
All as remembered – plum and lilac hedge,
tall laneside elm, rose trellis,
the leafy ranks of the potato patch.

A woman lifting her arms to the washing line
froze to stillness as the great dark warplane
swept thunderously above her head, its shadow
large as the whole lawn.

After, she'd have run indoors, sat steadying
her breath beneath the low red roof,
while we flew over Wickham Market – spire, pub,
bakery, the old waterpump in the square –

and on to Yorkshire. We'd been flying all day
above sights of waste and surrender –
Cologne's smoke-dark cathedral,
the ruined bridges of the Ruhr trailing rust.

# A Widowhood

She's wrinkled, busy, prim; nothing
of the recluse, though alone there
behind white walls, with the ash tree,
the taskmaster lawns.

She pours tea by the fire,
prosaic in a room that's a shrine,
polished and dusted, decked
with small collected ornaments,
a few well-framed photographs.
Battle of Britain histories
lie to hand on a low table;
slips of paper, worn soft, mark
the pages where she reads his name.

Above the mantel her icon,
the clear oils of a Kennington portrait;
head and shoulders larger than life,
battledress, gold-embroidered wings,
young flesh, young dedicated eyes
gazing beyond the chair she sits in.

She wore the same blue, sank drink for drink,
spoke fighter-pilot slang, revelled
(it was long ago) in a hero's bed
and laughed off clownish Death cavorting
at the sunlit airfield's edge until
one of his jokey strokes knocked
the Spitfire out of the sky.

## Wings

*(for John Drax Williams)*

Every autumn, scuffing leaves as I walk,
I see again a city park;
that resolute long-legged stride.
There's his hair, truly brown.
Dark eyes. A great Welsh nose.
Lips warmly red, sensuous, humorous.
A boy of twenty ripening towards...

Went into the drink we used to say
as if it meant a death soon over;
but he had to wait it out,
ditched on a bitter sea, the sky
soundless until too late.
A Johnny-in-the-cloud, his bones
found no home ground.

At autumn, fifty autumns now,
when dry leaves drift and spread
a rustling tide the coming rains
will silence and spread thin,
it's youth I come upon
unchanged in memory's reliquary.
Youth; not to be faced,
the black mouth, unslaked.

# 3   COME AWAY

# The Gate

A gull flew low across the garden
his spread sails white as washing
against blue sky on a good drying day

and I was back in Mevagissey, the wings
and cries, and the houses so close
that clothes are pegged high,

strung out from upper windows
on line and pulley to catch the air.
One day, standing for a moment

at the kitchen door I caught sight
of something half submerged moving along
the channel that ran to the harbour

through the backyards of that street.
It was some thing of yours lost days before
into the stream at the head of the valley

delivered home by water
with such nicety of coincidence.
What it was escapes me now.

Was it orange coloured, a size
to fit the palm? What weight and shape?
The searching has opened another closed gate.

There you are, not a hair lost; and the man
who was our child is flaxen again, naked,
laughing down from a forbidden rock.

The beach was yellow then before
the nightstorm that drew the sand away
dispersed its grains under the sea.

# Near Neighbours

In this house the turnover of crockery
has been as perceptible over the years
as the rotation of crops in a familiar field.
Blue-banded cups and saucers, ethnic
brown beakers that wore rough at the lip,
then supermarket mugs variously decorated –
mock-Victorian advertisements for corsets
or sewing machines rubbing sides with clusters
of crudely-bright fruit, wide red poppies,
or butterflies or a circle of Valentine hearts
and LOVE IS ...

The china in the other house never changes.
The family drinks from shapely cups,
eats from flute-edged plates until flower
and leaf emerge. A meal over, the dresser
bears again on every hook and shelf, blooms
carefully lustrous from suds and teatowel.
Throughout a marriage (and never an interloper
from Lawley's or the Co-op given houseroom)
the subtle pinks and greens have shone
beneath a pale glaze, uniform and uncrazed.
Each cloned rose could be last month's
replacement or a survivor from the first
purchase still unscathed.

I visit the other house, but am always glad
to be back home, amongst ephemera.
A teabag steeps in the stained cylinder
of my currently-favoured porcelain mug
printed with apples whole and halved.
I stir to tease out strength, spoon up
the sodden bag, add milk. Drinking,
listening to silence, I wonder
if my neighbours' children will be gardeners,
grow standard roses along straight paths;
wonder what harm or good will have stemmed
from my haphazard table, the brown clay,
the garish unvalued poppies.

# Window

Sometimes, everyone in bed,
she would need to flit across
the lit landing in the night,
go down a few stairs
to the lavatory, her face
blank with sleep, hair a dulled
fuzzed halo, a little barefoot figure
hurrying in a nightdress.
The long window that in daylight
showed apple leaves and sky
faced her, a black mirror.
There a lonely ghost child
stepped towards her
turned, when she turned,
as if to descend the stair
and then was left behind,
contained where the frame ended,
the wall's solidity began.

Returning, her cold soles
quick on the hard floor, she knew
though she did not risk a look,
that at the head of the stairs
the other child would have come again,
only to retreat, to run
into the depth behind the glass.
Fear fingering its spine,
nightdress folds flowing back,
it would be running
away along phantom floorboards
to where treetops were drowned
in the brimming dark
of the looking-glass garden.

# Changes

Will you *come to* church, will *you? Come* to church *will you...*
Come *on* then!  Come *on* then!  Come *on* then!
*Come    come    come    come    come    come.*

The sound is so loud on Sunday mornings
the whole town cannot help but hear.
But it's only the faithful
who respond, and they
were ready-dressed and hatted
and out on the pavements
before the first note chimed,
christian soldiers marching sedately
churchward to the familiar call
to receive comfort, offer praise.
Praise! Does God thrive on it,
need it to make him kind?

On Wednesday evenings
the ringers practise.
Waterfalls of sound tumble
from the tower,
flood every street
and garden with cadences,
triumphant clashings.
Calling upon no one,
they put the bells
through their paces,
assail our weekday ears
for an hour exactly
of concerted sweat and skill.

# Commonplace Man

A man I knew, a handyman, a mender,
who could tack down carpets, fix
locks and leaking taps, died in a game
of badminton, in what had seemed his prime.

Now as I go about the streets
of this town where he lived
I see him often walking towards me,
expect his customary greeting –
'All right, then?' Never uttered.
It's a stranger that approaches, passes by.

A commonplace man he must have been,
since I see his likeness not only
near to home but in distant places
he surely never visited. He strolls
along a city pavement, stares across
railway lines from an opposite platform.

Easily, often, his ghost comes,
someone not dear or close to me,
while my mourned dead withhold
their presences, even from dreams.

# Customer

Her hands are soft as the muslin
I imagine she wore as a girl.
They flutter, touching gently,
clasping my wrist for a moment,
brushing my arm like moth-wings.

Her fingers stroke velvets,
silvery brocades. She means
to make cushions and screens;
plans, she tells me, to stitch
nineteen tapestries, each

a twelvemonth's work...
who (she least of all)
can count on nineteen years,
or nine, or even one?
The canvases wait in a chest,

with her hoard of still-virgin
lengths of cloth –
succumbed-to temptations.
She never sews at all, I'm sure,
but only thinks of it –

making seams and pipings,
stitching unending flowers
in many coloured wools
across the framed mesh –
all in her head.

Of course she'll come again,
admire more pieces, smooth them
lovingly with her moth hands,
and take them home, her mind
bee-busy with ideas.

# All-Steel Traveller

It might have been from childhood loyalty
(my boat-race favour always the dark blue)
that I bought her, fifth-hand Morris Oxford.
Solid, I thought, a workhorse – then
I came across the leaflet. On holiday,
streamlined, she almost flies uphill.
Another scene – five grown-ups setting off;
a bow-tied flunkey loads their luggage.
Everybody smiles. The children wave goodbye.
Lastly, a light task; boss and shirtsleeved help
lift flower-boxes to the tailgate.

*The New All-Steel Traveller. Robust.*
*colourful, handsome, the most accommodating*
*and versatile multi-purpose car ever.*
But a heavy weight to push on mornings
of low battery and damp air. And garage-men
despise cars that are out-of-date,
not veteran or vintage. Spare parts
accruing interest on warehouse shelves
began to cost more than seemed reasonable.

*Complete Comfort. Famous Oxford Vigour.*
*Space to stow more – and more...*
I could have saved her.
New engine, new whatever-else she needed,
bright-chromed and glossily resprayed,
that old lady might have done me proud –
a head-turner, a pristine rarity,
patient in cities, brave on motorways,
steadily taking rough and smooth.
We might have been co-travellers still

except that I lacked courage, took
the paltry price. Steel scrap. Five tyres...
They fixed a rope. A man in oil-steeped shoes
slid in behind the wheel.
She rolled away, soundlessly.

# Lanhydrock's People

The avenue stretches away, narrowing towards distant trees,
straight and safe but leading, like an avenue in a novel,
to dangerous highways.

How they must have spanked away, all gloss and jingle,
a stylish exit from a stage where every prop's in place –
every magnolia tree and copper pan, the household
spotlessly smocked or aproned for farewell,
poised to sustain the master's absence.

And the return – the house growing greater
with every equine stride, windows plenished
like amber; the gathering of dignity's reserves
within the wrenched and muddied carriage
as it circled the courtyard to the opening door,
to warmth and rest. Yet even as the homecomers slept
their solid beds would seem to rock and lurch,
take on the journey's rhythms, just for a night or two

until the powerful calm house could overcome illusion –
its beeswaxed floors demonstrating smoothness,
stillness; furniture standing steady; the carers
absorbed again in rituals of hearth and table.

# Levitation

The sailing above roof and steeple
was as real to them as the aromatics
they stroked along each limb and into
the body's planes and crevices, real
as the specifics held on the tongue
and swallowed before each flight.

In grey first light, straining to lift
beyond this bedroom ceiling,
I will my self to where you are,
hours westward of this sunrise –
will you to wake and question, to recognise
the thrall of hallucinogens potent

as drug or ointment. Love. Obsession.
You could be eagle or gull, or angel poised
on summer's melting clouds as if on a rooted summit
and I fear you may be flying only to fall
from those heights you write of in letters
that reach me eight days stale.

# The Man Across the Road

Almost every day he emerges
dangling a shopping bag –
square and flat; hardly more rounded
when he comes home.

He walks with the bent-kneed
forward slope of old age, as if life
were a marathon in slow motion.
His hasty days are over.

Once he fixed roof-trusses, lintels,
clambered around building sites,
a cricket of a man. Still chirpy,
he greets me across the roadway,

a row of china teeth smiling
almost liplessly, eyes moist and alive
above the delicate flush that warms
the network of his cheeks

and one hand raised towards the brim
of a weather-stained trilby hat.
Last winter his wife died;
the front-room grate stayed cold.

He wouldn't sit on his own
facing that chair like an empty lap
on the other side of the hearth.
Now, early dark again, his window

once more answers mine. I glimpse
flame between his skimpy curtains,
and the rainbow flicker of television –
its many voices requiring

no more in reply than did she –
the gossip, the street's nosey one.
I guess that, after a year of it,
he's had enough of silence.

## Polruan, September

I watch a man set out, his woollen hat
defying the morning cold. He pauses on the path,
searches an inner breast pocket, goes on
down the stone flight that links the terraces,
coughing and puffing smoke – a not-young
working man, his bowed legs stiff until the day
eases them. A tortoiseshell cat watches too.
Precarious on a shed's slippery roof
she contemplates a leap.

Below in the still estuary a corps de ballet
of small craft awaits curtain-up, all turned
as if toward some distant audience inland.
Each glides with its upturned partner –
blue boat on blue, red on red, white
on dove grey. The water's gunmetal,
darkening to old pewter beneath the far cliffs.

The ferryboat with its flounce of old tyres
sets off without passengers, its wide-cast
wake defined by twisting ropes of water.
Too early yet for the day's first voyagers
to work or school across the river.

Mist lifts, melts into the sky above Fowey.
The estuary basks in sunlight. Where did I see grey?
The cliffs' reflections are pale ochre; the houses'
coloured likenesses stretch half across the river.
Now each white hull floats on an aqueous lily,
a more golden self. All seem new-painted, primary,
moving in unison as if to music when a cargo boat
sweeps by, leaving on the tide.

# Newlyn School

Boys sit in a row atop the harbour arm.
Their shirts are collarless handed-downs,
punished by dolly and washboard,
their breeches rough-hemmed at the knee –
the cloth of their fathers' trousers,
whatever's left to sew after long wearing.

Summer has bleached their hair,
dusted the bare legs that dangle
calf and heel against the salty granite.
They're waiting to gather the leavings,
for the boats to come sliding alongside,
the catch thrown down, pollock and catfish
that flop and skid on a quay
soon scale-slimed and awash.
All that's here as yet is a soundless sky
and distant sails, and the boys waiting.
An artist, an incomer, painted them.

A century on; now the boats trawl for scarcer shoals,
come throbbing to the dockside, unawaited.
The children, in shop-bought clothes, dryshod,
climb school hill to a new term.
The world has become their village; they know
of its poisoned waters, vanished forests, thinning sky.
They make pictures, write verses; glean worry.

# Frontier

They'd built the single track, set the train
climbing and descending, all seasons
between snows, first for long-skirted ladies
with their escorts and their sketchbooks;

that day for us. We were almost strangers –
a travellers' encounter on the express
southbound through the St Gotthard.
Now we stood on Monte Generoso's height.

Spreading to one horizon lay flat Lombardy –
farmland, uncounted cypresses; on the other hand
beyond lake and valley, poised it seemed
free of Earth, the far high mountains rose

through opalescent mists to a flawless sky,
robed to their crowns in light. Tears,
uncheckable as rain, spilled from my eyes.
He stayed beside me, silent, unembarrassed.

All afternoon we sat on, lulled, replete
with spectacle, turned towards the plain.
The popple of bells lifted through thin warm air
and other, rhythmic, sounds – at last interpreted.

Somewhere below us and above the plain
a sentry marched. We heard at even intervals
the jangle of arms, his tread coming and going,
marking the unchallenged frontier.

# Lugano

At the last moment, stretching up,
she put a scrap of paper from a notebook page
into the hand that reached from the moving window.
The night train had begun to slide away,
first seconds of its passage – Switzerland, France,
then London, where she too would soon return;
and where, though walking the same city,
they might not have met again.

Now she must sort his things.
The wallet leather's soft from daily use.
Money, receipts, used tickets, and her own
young face, creased, rubbed dull. Then
from a pocket meant perhaps for stamps
a small soiled square she knows at once,
though twentyseven years have passed,
is scribbled with a number and a name.


# Lostwithiel

We wait at a level crossing; sunshine
through the car window hot
on the green sleeve of my dress.
The baby's asleep; we're in no hurry.
A moment of recall – nothing much,
except...
                    now I know
what I miss most, the worst lack
for the rest of life – the warmth
that without any touch
the scent that without any
perceptible odour his presence
wrapped around me – the thing
that hovers and is gone:
happiness.

## Pair-Bond

The children play in the garden
where I sit, their mother. I am thus.
He comes home – and I am other.
I walk alone in the street; I'm thus.
He's my companion – other.
The bed seems bare until he
slides in against me
cold-skinned from a winter journey.

When he's there, recalled,
it's as if my molecules even now
respond to a lost polarity.
There's a memory of peace
beyond regaining.

Eighteen years since,
and the bond still holds.


## A Brave Face

We had each evolved
masks kind to the other –
you cheerfully walking the pavements
of a city you could not admire;
I hiding a frantic dismay.
The blisters on your heels were raw;
you wore first one pair of shoes
then another, then the first again.

We made no tourist round.
It was only afterwards and alone
I entered the Jeu de Paume.


84

One night we ate poor food
in a sawdust-strewn Left Bank café,
the next dined richly
on our last francs.

If we could live it again
I'd not let you wear so brave a face.
They give me pain still,
those unhealed feet of yours
now ten years turned to ash.

## Nil Desperandum...

The tide was already ebbing,
to lay bare the truth I shrank from
and he chose to disregard.
How should he have used time,
dealt a death sentence,
no term set on the interim?

We lived it out as he wanted,
our text one of his mottoes –
*take no notice.* Long-used,
like *fuck the neighbours*;
and the unspoken one –
*never apologise.* Make a will,
the doctor said. Get your affairs
in order. I knew he wouldn't.

His way was not to protect
but always to test my mettle.
I guess he thought me strong enough
to deal with what would come,
stand up to any bastard
who might try to grind me down.

# Leaving the Party

At two o'clock, the last full moon of the year,
the night immaculate, starchy with frost,
I stood in the square of gold
thrown with the noise of talk and music
across the silent air
onto the leaves of sleeping bushes.
I took in my hand
a finial bud of rhododendron
closely bound in a brown tissue
like cloth from the Egyptian dead,
like the stained graveclothes
of all who hoped to live again
listening to the words
of Isis or Jesus.

# Come Away

His name
filled my scream
I ran barefoot down the stairs
fast as the childhood dream

when lions follow;
up again I ran,
the stairs a current of air
blew me like thistledown.

I laid my palm on his calf
and it was warm and muscled
and like life.

Come away said the kind doctor.
I left the body there
lying straight, our wide bed
a single bier.

All night I watched
tree branches scratch the sky,
printed another window-frame
for ever on my eye.

When I came home in the morning
all the warmth had gone.
I touched his useless hand.
Where his eyes had shone
behind half-lifted lids were grown
cataracts of stone.

# When You Died

### 1

When you died
I went through the rain
carrying my nightmare
to register the death.

A well-groomed healthy gentleman
safe within his office
said – Are you the widow?

Couldn't he have said
Were you his wife?

### 2

After the first shock
I found I was
solidly set in my flesh.
I was an upright central pillar,
the soft flesh melted round me.
My eyes melted
spilling the inexhaustible essence of sorrow.
The soft flesh of the body
melted onto chairs and into beds
dragging its emptiness and pain.

I lodged inside holding myself upright,
warding off the dreadful deliquescence.

3

November.
Stooping under muslins
of grey rain I fingered
through ribbons of wet grass,
traced stiff stems down to the wormy earth
and one by one snapped off
the pale surviving flowers; they would ride
with him, lie on the polished plank
above his breast.

People said – Why do you not
follow the coffin?
Why do you not
have any funeral words spoken?
Why not
send flowers from a shop?

4

When you died
they burnt you.
They brought home to me
a vase of thin metal;
inside, a plastic bag
crammed, full of gritty pieces.
Ground bones, not silky ash.

Where shall I put this substance?
Shall I scatter it
with customary thoughts
of nature's mystical balance
among the roses?

Shall I disperse it into the winds
that blow across Cambeake Cliff
or drop it onto places where you
lived, worked, were happy?

Finally shall I perhaps keep it
which after all was you
quietly on a shelf
and when I follow
my old grit can lie
no matter where with yours
slowly sinking into the earth together.


5

When you died
I did not for the moment
think about myself;
I grieved deeply and purely for your loss,
that you had lost your life.
I grieved bitterly for your mind destroyed,
your courage thrown away,
your senses aborted under the amazing skin
no one would ever touch again.

I grieve still
that we'd have grown
even more deeply close and old together
and now shall not.

## Two Years

When you died
all the doors banged shut.

After two years, inch by inch,
they creep open.
Now I can relish
small encounters,
encourage
small flares of desire;
begin to believe as you did
things come right.
I tell myself that you
escaped the slow declension to old age
leaving me to indulge
this wintry flowering.

But I know
it's not like that at all.

## Four Years

The smell of him went soon
from all his shirts.
I sent them for jumble,
and the sweaters and suits.
The shoes
held more of him; he was printed
into his shoes. I did not burn
or throw or give them away.
Time has denatured them now.

Nothing left.
There will never be
a hair of his in a comb.
But I want to believe
that in the shifting housedust
minute presences still drift:
an eyelash,
a hard crescent cut from a fingernail,
that sometimes
between the folds of a curtain
or the covers of a book
I touch
a flake of his skin.


## Five Years


These are not desired or indulged tears;
acid, insistent, they have harassed my eyelids
all day, and now in the room where he died
they fall like leaves falling
without volition or noise.

Recall after recall comes, single moments
free from the motives, the confusions
of circumstance that forced us
to waste ourselves and our
time; they pour through my memory,
still do not make a pattern.

The summit of grief is passed. How
do I learn to live with the helpless rage,
begin to accept death's barren truth?
Hand in hand go disbelief and the fear
of my own moment to come, rankling
like the fear of the first
act of love
the first parturition.

## Coming to Terms

In nearly thirty years he would not say
he loved me. At first I found it hard
having to believe without the words
my upbringing had led me to expect

that he did indeed desire
and need me enough to have gladly
abandoned all others for my sake.
In vulnerable moments I might dare

rashly to ask the forbidden question;
he was adamant, allowing me only
the explanation that, for him,
the word had become debased,

currency of cheap fiction designed
to daze the half-literate. No use
evoking Donne and Shakespeare;
other times, other values.

Growing in love for him, perforce unspoken,
I came to see his reticence as trust,
as tribute to my strength.
The approach of death also

we faced silently, on his terms.
You might say now I have liberty of speech.
Through unshared rooms year after year
I spin words. At first they all

seemed precious, each of intrinsic value.
Now I see they are threads that anyone
may weave; worth's in fine cloth,
a warm coat sewn to fit.

# View from the Train

St Mary Reddecliffe's spire; beneath it
we'd talked of Chatterton, ill-fated clever boy,
and the romantic deathbed painting in the Tate.
No thought then of real death, the capricious
equaliser, unequally removing.

My brown boy, my soft-hearted
hard-willed man, you also were not meant
to grow weak-thighed, to totter and fumble.
I have learned this, watching old men
slow walking, nodding as they talk
and smile purple-lipped at their deaf
wrinkled wives. Well, we shall not
see each other so degraded,
you unknowing now, me travelling on.

# A Love Poem

There were two that mattered. Two.
Better than one only, or many small,
or none, the heart's desert.

Pain comes afterwards, when it's done,
can't ever be again, the full hunger
that nothing quite assuages,

the reaching that never quite touches,
the welling up never contained, brimmed
wastefully. Our bodies are less than enough

for the need to give. Eyes, speech, nakedness,
clasped hands, all die with flesh, but love
keeps growing like a genie, endlessly

pouring from the pinched neck of dark glass,
crying out – You did not ask enough.
There could have been more, more.


## The Road


On a day dappled with bright cumulus
I thought myself distanced enough
by years and the season to trace
his November journey.

Butterflies, warm air, the claytips
shining white beyond green hedges –
none of these had enriched
that solitary walk.

He'd have stepped quickly,
shrugged into his sheepskin coat.
I know the swing of his thighs,
how his feet touched ground

as he strode through the last
hours of his life, saying goodbye
to the world, light, time –
himself.
            Yes, there was something

shared after – a meal, a conversation,
or how would I know of the road and how far
he walked, and who it was (chance-met)
who drove him home?

# The Atheist

They laid him like a saint
arms X-shaped on his breast
a pose of holiness.
Past reason or protest

in death he's made to suit
the customary norm –
the plank's convenience,
grave width and coffin form.


# In the Morning

Cloud moves across the skylight.
The curve of the stairwell wall
is a pale backdrop. They ease down
the splayed steps where the treads
are narrowest, leaning their weight
on the banister rail as they lug him,
naked, chin slumped to pallid chest.

The lower man grasps the knees,
the other, palms hitched in the armpits,
has to stoop, taking the greater strain.
They reach the flat of the landing
where I stand caught in a doorway,
stockstill with shock. Eyes averted,
they bundle past, turn and go on
down the easier straight staircase.

Will they shield him – box or shroud –
when they reach the door?

Give me no ceremony, he'd said;
Yet I observe aghast this wounding passage;
the last of him, who yesterday I saw
running the length of the street.

# The Silence

A set of tomes about volcanoes –
valuable perhaps. Textbooks
on engineering, maths, geology.
I piled them up, apart
from those we'd jointly owned:
our large-size art-books
(post-impressionists); Joyce,
Kafka, Dostoyevsky. Some
had been his, some mine –
*À la recherche du temps perdu,*
unread beyond volume four.

Then at the back this folder,
boards warped, leaves
rusted around the rings.
Poems. I sat and read.

All the exigencies of our years
stood between me, now,
and those unrequited verses
written before we met.
He'd kept them, like old letters;
like, indeed, my old love's letters
never thrown away – keepsakes
of something not fulfilled
but not regretted.

I set my hand flat on the surfaces
he'd touched – and no one since.
I held my cheek
against the written pages.
Did we each thwart the other's muse,
demand, and take, too much?
Or was it that we drank
from a filled cup
from which no poems spilled?

# Rayden on Divorce (Fifth Edition)

Bought in a mixed auction-lot a black-bound book,
four pounds in weight, for years stood on a shelf –
unopened but deserving of its space.
When we came close to quarrelling one of us,
mostly the less indignant, would point
towards the title on its spine; sham threat –
both of us deeply sure that Rayden's specialty
was something we'd not need.

Now, sorting possessions, what to keep,
I take it down, leaf through.
The Table of Cases, Abbott through Zycklinski,
fills ninety pages, a close-printed list
of partners counterposed. I learn that Gold
was freed from Gold (nineteen-o-eight),
Silver and Silver parted (eighteen-seventy),
Shorthouse got rid of Shorthouse – on and on
thousands of paired genderless names, un-paired.

Terse headings subdivide the chapters:
*Pleadings. Wilful Refusal. Past Offences.*
*Sterility No Ground. Costs. Damages.*
*Connivance.* More than two hundred years
of precedents are here – prayers and rulings,
pitfalls and denials, a catalogue of severances
sought or endured, arrived at by slow process.

Ours was immediate, absolute; not sought by either,
not decreed by any court of law.

## Visitation

Only once has he come to me in a dream,
approaching across the grey yard by the garden.
He seemed suddenly to be there, but perhaps
had been waiting in the shade of the wall.
Nearer by two or three steady steps he came,
his arms not reaching, parallel, seeking,
but spread wide, angled toward me from the shoulder.
Palms open he mutely offered himself.

That was the whole of the dream, the one
gift from the other side of death.


## Exorcists

I don't tell my guests –
they sleep sound and wake smiling,
draw back new curtains to the morning

bringing in daylight. The carpet's new, too,
everything is, even the white-framed window
that shuts out the rain.

The floorboards no longer weep.
Surely beneath the plain brown pile
the old wood is as dry now

as seaside timber in a July heat.
Aired linen celebrates each innocent head.
The amnesiac walls are clean as milk.

# Horoscope, September

Capricorn: not my sign
nor the sign of anyone I know.
There's no future in reading
forecasts for Capricorn.

Sagittarius; this month it seems
we merit a visit overseas. A sexual gamble
will pay off before October.
For every one of us? I wonder
about the sexually gambling sagittarian
infants and octogenarians
(and have they got the spelling right?).

Sagittarius this month must watch
for wishful thinking in love. This
I shall try to do, shall not turn
to Capricorn's horoscope.
There is no January man
now in my life.

# Small Comfort

The day is shadowed over by your grief.
Drained by your tears, I have only this,
that you can not accept, to give.

From the lip of my own scaled pit
I tell you –
Slowly, never perfectly,
even against the will,
time heals.

## Seven Years

When I was newly wounded by his death
the voice came nightly; as I drowsed it called
high, single in my head, one note
that dragged me out of drift. It was no word
but a short human sound, close, clear as oboe,
calling as if to sleep were dangerous,
too much like death itself. Night after night
it hauled me back, forbade me the soft slide
towards the desired, anonymous, abyss.
Who called? Was it to injure or to warn?
Did I myself cry out?
                              This morning early
a shrill bell woke me. Half-asleep I groped
to silence it. But silence was already whole
as a healed scar, and no real clock was there.


## Nine Years

Still there, in rooms we shared,
on roads we travelled. He leans
on the kitchen counter, drinking coffee;
he writes, reads, walks, smiles

but never speaks. If he could speak
or hear I might give him more
than these hopeless tears that still
fall at thought of him.

I strive so to get answer –
wordlessly, since he has no words –
but my desire can surge no further
than my forehead's boundary

and no answer comes, nothing at all.
Only my own thousand thousand images
of place and movement remain with me,
unrenewable, grief-heavy, ghost-light.


## The Twentieth Year


In the middle of a field a woman
stands talking to a man – as if she
were the landowner. A silky brown bear cub
on either arm – she sets them down.
They're off down the slope
towards the wood.

We stand a moment in the gateway
to a farmer's drive, watch
as a helicopter comes in low.
There's a plane in the home meadow.
How the country's changed!
It's clean as new paint.

So long since –
yet it's as if our companionship
had never been ruptured.
We're walking to catch a train.
OK for time, you say. Then,
See! – as we top a rise and there's
the pink brick of the station wall,
the railway logo.

The northbound train is in,
full of darkclothed people,
plump middle-aged women
in frowsty black, rustic men.
We jostle across to the other platform,
are crowded towards a carriage.

I'm in and you step up – I see your foot
on the step. I've kept two seats
with a spread of our Sunday papers.
The train pulls out, goes rocking on;
you're not there.

I wake weeping.
Thankyou, thankyou, I say
over and over.

## Time

This is a room he never saw
in a house in a city
we sometimes travelled through.

The wool of my dress
the leather of my shoes
still grew as pasture while he lived.

My skin's new-celled, my body
set with new-sprung
nails and hair.

It's said that while flesh
lasts to nourish it a man's beard
grows on in the tomb – but his

was consumed in an hour.
In a box in this room I keep
his dry unchanging ash.

# Write

Write, and there's certainly
something there – a sorrow,
a celebration – but never
rich or full enough, never
dredged so deeply that it scours
the bowl of the pelvis, wrenches
at every last reserve of breath.

Can't, can't, love or mourn
to the extreme in words.
I remember the ignition
of flesh, and the comfort of it;
remember as if the loss were new –
or believe I do. The ache
permeates viscera, marrow –

how make that ring true?
How translate the heart
(if that's the vessel of love)
into lines and sentences
or tell of chance sights or sounds
that stir old cindered griefs
to harsh momentary heat.

# 4 DRIVING TO THE LAKE

# Bognor, 1947

We arrived with our separate suitcases.
There was no mistaking the manager's
misgivings. He informed us firmly

that our allotted rooms were distanced
by the full length of the corridor
and on different floors. We dined quietly

across near-white damask. Even now
I remember brown meat in heavy gravy,
gloss-painted cream walls, curtains

stiff as chain-mail, the hard eyes
of the waitress and the boss
forbidding in conjunction.

Resentment healed as we travelled,
leaving the coast behind.
The inn's tiled roof spread wide

like mothering wings. We were given keys
to two attic rooms with a shared stair,
a carpeted landing.

# Spencer Park

A saffron autumn, hardly any red
or russet, or brown yet;
leaves bleached in random patterns
lighten daily to melon-ripeness,
soft as sleepy pears.

Rising from waves of scumbled
darkly green gorse, dormant,
sparsely sparked with bloom,
a copse of silver birches
tosses up fountains of small yellow flames,
celebrates the ending
of the late Indian summer.

At evening under lanterns strung from boughs
we eat and drink and stand wet-soled
in grass unnaturally emerald.
Candle flames trapped in jars
dwindle along paths.
Children wheel about in coltish herds
full of night-freedom, the excitement
of flame-ferns curling,
red sparks tracer-shooting
through the slow waltz of the climbing smoke.

Fireworks, crackling torrents of white and coloured light,
will not live so gentle in the mind
as the warm bonfire cavern scooped out of the dark
or as the slow daylight burning
of the birch trees' living leaves.


## Perspective


Sometimes I still catch glimpses:
a village of tile or thatch
or a single farmhouse, comfit logs
stacked in the yard, matchbox tractor
scoring a slow brown furrow
and orchards studded with pinhead
fruit, amber and ruby –
all distant perfect miniatures.

It's a landscape of few people.
Still remembered from years ago
a figurine in white apron
running from a cottage door to chase
chickens that scattered across the yard,
so small a sparrow could have pecked them up.
And even last week the train halted
outside a country station on an embankment
fuzzy with the poised seeds of willowherb
and there below was a little group
quite self-absorbed, in their dolls' house
garden chairs, taking tea on a sunny lawn.

Yes, of course I know it's imagination,
a trick of distance, but sometimes
so convincing that mimic world appears,
with its sheep and cars and cricket fields
that I fall to wondering from what hill,
what carriage window, the Dean
first caught sight of Lilliput.


## Hot Day on the Motorway


Brilliance and drought.
Illusion lacquers each rise.
A black wing glued to the fast lane
flaps as if alive.

No spark of bloom to be seen
in mile after mile
of driving between verges massed
with gorse – an adage disproved;

kissing's in season, gorse-flowers
or none, though not all
are kissed, not all are born sound
or comely, or are loved;

108

not all live to be old. I count
my blessings. Hay-sweet air streams
against my face; the seat's sweaty hold
is safe, familiar. But suddenly new

and colder drops spring on lip
and spine – the traffic sweeps aside
like shoaling minnows to make way.
Siren and flashing beam

pull level, rush by. On the road ahead
a browning stain compacts the dust;
bone cringes against steel, both
irreparable. Slowing as we go past

we stare furtively, to glimpse
a scatter of headlamp glass crushed
like sugar-candy, a shape on the grass
shrouded from toe to crown.

Beneath the blanket are cooling eyes
blind to the mesh of threads, mouth
without breath to cloud a mirror. We touch
wood, cross fingers, drive on.

## 16.19 from Exeter

We edge out above the city's two streams, river
and canal – the one rippled, flowing, the other opaque,
a slide where ducks falter, a daring boy runs.

Goal-posts identify a printless football field.
Then iced meadows, a trotting dog, a man singular
as an exclamation mark. Sheep fleeced in brown
scatter, grains on a damask cloth.

The land folds away. We beat the shore's bounds.
A snowy froth crusts the ocean's edge. No line
marks sea from sky; each grey consumes the other.
Crested breakers rage out of a blur of cloud.
We flash past a halt, whitespread boards untrodden.
From the lip of the sea-wall a sudden flight of gulls
hurls upward, soundless beyond our glass.

Yellow lights blink on Teignmouth bridge.
Still-salt water laps along the track's low bank.
We follow the estuary, its grey mudflats bleached.
The sweetening river's margins are hard in ice,
sealed from the stalking curlews.

At Newton Abbot we slide through a fan of tracks.
Lit platform and frosted town approach, slip away
into dusk. Forehead pressed to the window
I distinguish the soil's patterns – ribbed fields
and mottled pasture dark through a skim of white.

And then a new thickness of snow glimmers
beneath our night-mirrored carriage. Sledged ghosts
on either hand speed with us through the cold.


## Banquette in the Hotel Metropole


The mounds between the dimples
shine garnet-red, pollened
with tungsten-yellow light.

Empty. You leaned yesterday
against the padded velvet.
Now it looks plumply virgin

as if yesterday had never been.
Whore of a seat, it welcomes
all comers equally. Today's strangers

110

and tomorrow's will come, to sink
through your after-image into comfort,
to sit, quiet or animated,

dinting the plush, warming it
one after another to human heat.
Each morning, the brush,

the vacuum cleaner. Next year
perhaps I shall love
someone else.


## Inside Out


Roll-out-the-barrel nights,
years ago, we roistered
along the pubby alleys of Downalong
while sashes rattled up and out wagged
night-cuffed fists and shouting heads.
*'Get home you youngsters.*
*Leave people sleep.'*

Now I walk through labyrinths
of memory. Venice has overlaid St Ives,
given her a heart of water.
My mind recasts the map,
refuses the sense of promontory.

I look for the snake-curve of a channel
that must be bridged or sailed.
But there's no Grand Canal –
the sea flanks the land;
the town's spine is solid.
Step by step
I must learn it again.

## At Knossos

*(March 1984)*

The dolphins in the queen's chamber
swim eagerly across the wall.
The doorways are outlined
in flowery medallions, and the queen's
flush lavatory is no more primitive
than those we visited briefly
by the ticket office.

The tub she bathed in would,
we're told, have been filled for her
with milk or sparkling wine.
It's small, a rounded oblong,
made for the child size
of that powerful, rich,
Minoan lady.

Fire swept away her courts
but the little bath remains.
It stirs our wonder,
set where hands can't reach
to wear its rim by touching –
a terracotta Lazarus
raised only to be cloistered.

At Knossos the dolphins, lilies,
bulls and princes have been drawn
from fragments of the ruined whole;
deduced, imagined. Was this indeed
a royal bath, or was it common cistern,
sink, or kneading-trough – or manger
from the dark hub of the maze?

*Envoi 1991*

Slightly shameful, like an end-of-garden loo,
the old convenience stood behind dark bushes,
a limewashed outhouse, unattended.

Near the new entrance are the new facilities.
The queue waits in a passage with tiled walls.
Drachmae are dropped into an outstretched hand,
thin squares of paper offered in return –
passport to a row of pristine cubicles,
doors swinging open, swinging shut.


## Souda Bay

I'm not great on cemeteries, I said;
but when we got there had to walk away
alone, so moved by the white headstones
that marked where young bones lay
beneath long weedless beds set out with flowers.
Boats drowsed across the bay. A dry air
soundlessly stirred the eucalyptus leaves.
The sky was enamel blue, a bright veneer.

Two gardeners mowed the already-perfect grass
and heavy fruit fell from trimmed orange-trees.
There were no mounds, no grave-shaped burials,
only the shoulder-to-shoulder monuments,
identities engraved – or to record
the nameless, a laconic *Known to God.*

# Dredger

Porridges of insoluble sludge
scooped from the estuary floor
slap through her open deck.

A sluice of thin mud drains down
from the climbing panniers, streaks her
with earth colours, dun, ochre.

Pulsing, she gnaws at seabed drifts,
at moulded barriers of sand. Sometimes
we see the grey eye-stalk of a submarine

sliding across the bay's blue waters.
Evenings, the tavernas are full
of young sailors out of uniform

and the dredger's off-duty,
her clattering stilled, her rusty bulk
at ease in the harbour's dark embrace.

# Venetian Red

We wake beneath a ceiling dark as olives.
Along the top line of the shutters
a shallow ledge of daylight shows. Sunshine

can't touch this window, but will slant
onto the balcony obliquely opposite
where the old lady seems to sit all day

(we come and go beneath gestures of amity).
The heavy wooden leaves hinged back
we face a flatness of old stucco

and blinds still drawn behind glass.
Leaning towards our mirrored selves,
we look up for the weather, blue or cloud.

Then, like a sudden dawn, colour
floods our room. Sunlight, overtopping
the roofline, reaches into the narrow

rift of the canal, illuminates
wrought iron intricacies, fat plants
in pots, white hair and grey companion cat –

a clear April light that strikes her house
and, angled back to us, brings what it's borrowed
from her painted wall – a shade of ancient red.


## Vivaldi's Church


The April day cooled hours ago.
A dark wind sweeping in from the lagoon
sets wavelets slapping upon stone,
rocks the tethered gondolas. Late,
we hurry along alleys, across bridges.

The concert's begun. We wait on cold flags,
to catch a moment when a pause allows
a settling in. Full benches are ranked close
beneath a lofty painted firmament –
scrolls, clouds, saints, patriarchs,

and angels, floating draperies upheld
as if in an airy windless summer.
Across the unpillared space the four
blacksuited men, playing with unfeigned
pleasure, hold us absorbed, united.

Applause releases us between sonatas;
we stir, become aware of separateness,
and of the slippery narrow planks we sit on.
Against each of my thighs I feel another
soft thigh pressing, comfortable, sexless;

until the music soars again, and I'm simply
a listener – here now, if never again,
beneath the thronged dome where he
(maestro, Venezia's red-headed priest)
rested his gaze when he put aside his bow.


## Waterways


Along the Grand Canal, flurried
by criss-cross wakes, moored gondolas
peck with restless patrician beaks
at the still-cold April air.
Fashioned with a subtle list,
enamelled a shining black,
they toss and lurch against quays
where green weed answers
the suck and push of the stream.

Beside stone steps in a quiet fondamente
a gondolier crouches, carefully tracing
white scrolls onto a glossy prow, readying
for Easter's surge of tourists.

As yet the weather's a patchwork –
mornings when every ripple scintillates,
and then a seeping rain. Processions
of black umbrellas lift across bridges –
a hundred willow-pattern arcs.
But in this city of scarce soil no willow
finds roothold, all waterways hemmed in
by walls at one with their reflections –
villas and palaces upheld
on a forest of drowned trees.

## Coach Tour

We wait at the border post,
a concrete-slab guardhouse.
Ahead's a lawn made sparse
by beech shade, the grass
wet as the green slopes
we've passed through since
that so-early breakfast.

Flower-seeds and butterflies
drift across the invisible line.
We can see kittens playing there,
grown cats beneath a tree
grooming themselves clean
of the dust and blood
of last night's excursions.

Uniforms. Documents.
Our heads are counted;
perhaps we're vouched for.
The coach goes through.
We may step down now,
drink a morning coffee,
stroke the impartial cats.

# Floating

The sea deepens slowly,
glass–clear, strongly salt,
warm at summer's end.

I'm slung like a hammock
buoyed at head and toes.
A body-length below
my shadow, a still shape,
masks out the shimmering mesh
that nets the shallows.

Sunshine spills down
from the lap of the waves.
Across the slowly-mutable
ripples of seabed sand
flosses of lucent gold
weave and unweave, a tangle
of restless patternings.

Arms spread, I can hang
in the silk of the water
unmoving. My body's snakeskinned
with wavelight, traversed
by miniature suns,
each floating bubble
a cool lens of air.

# Fresh Bread

Late at night, the baker rests his weight.
The small hard chair's tilted back
alongside the shop's shadowy glass
where membraned packs of knobby biscuits
are heaped against the pane, a coral reef
of deep-sea creatures.
Streetlight slants on his great pale thighs,
bare and parted. The day-used apron,
belly-strings untied, drapes limply
between his knees to the sidewalk dust.

Morning, and freshly laundered white
smooths his girth, falls decorously
to below the hems of his drill shorts.
There's new bread on the shelves –
and long hot hours ahead, to fill
with rolls, pies, cakes that ooze honey.
Those stout thighs won't loll again
until evening, until stars
sugar the cooling sky.

[Crete, September 1991]

119

## Kalives – Morning

The neighbour cock, on his toes at any hour,
screeches all night at random intervals.
At last it's almost light.

Nightdressed, I stand in the yard, look out
past suntrap screens, half-ready houses,
power cables, pronged aerials,

towards the sea, the smooth wash of sky –
a flawless height and width of colour
shifting, deepening

until the sun's clean-edged disc
lifts behind the headland, fierce red
that counters red, lets in day-colours,

gold and blue. Suddenly I know
that my feet are cold, the concrete rough;
that traffic surges on the road below,

an early rush soon spent. A bitterness
stings my throat, the acrid organic stink
of burning wool, bones, feathers.

## Lucifer

*Kalives, September*


Daybreak; the unimaginable
fire's slowly unscreened –
bright and dangerous
as the fierce melt that, poured
from cup to mould,
focuses foundry darkness.
The headland's a dark whaleback;
pinpoint lamps gleam low on its flank
where a village wakes.

Flares of colour steep the sky,
fugitive crimson, milky vermilion,
pale rose and peachbloom; alloys
of liquid gold and copper
plate the black ocean.
Stars fade, vanish; but there's one –
a spark, no more, but resolute –
held to the last
in the lightening East.


## Light


The waves break ankle-low.
Flurries of darting fish
child's-finger sized, flick back
as the water spreads thin,
shallowing the living-space
between air and sand.
But they come in so close
to my wading feet that I see their twins –
the real creatures – almost translucent
above the swimming shadows.

After noon we sit in the shade.
On the far edge of the neighbouring
rough land – at night pulsing with cicadas,
by day dumbstruck, bathed in heat –
stand three dry seedheads on tall stems.
In the fierce light they're drained
of colour, near-invisible;
yet, clearer than substance,
their shape's a grey candelabrum
on the whitewashed wall.

[Crete, September 1991]


## Sweetcorn


There's a stir by the taverna.
People sit on the shaky iron chairs
or stand against a wall, heads bent,
hands lifted like mouth-organists.

Under the great tree a little crowd
presses around the corn-seller.
He plunges a muscular bare arm;
his brown churn's emptying fast,

the heads of grain drawn out, held
steaming in iron tongs, salted,
presented, paid for in small coin.
Plump honey-gold spirals of maize –

we gnaw until each cradle's emptied,
until on squares of thin damp paper
two cores lie on the rusty tabletop –
creamy artefacts, pocked ivory.

The extras drift away. Regulars
of two weeks' standing, we stay
for our evening ouzo, wait
for the return of appetite.


## The Season of Red


Bougainvillaea, tireless all summer,
still reaches high, falls
in tumbling fullness – butterfly bracts
of crimson, scarlet.

Geraniums hungry for water,
hibiscus flowering fresh each day
as if newly nourished, oleander
swaying at roadsides – these names

are known or learned easily
by word of mouth, from books.

Letter by letter I spell out
titles above shops, on trucks.
*Minotaurus* on the tailgate of a van,
*Apollo* above a cinema.

*Kalispera* we call, parrot-fashion,
passing old women at dusk.
*Kalispera* they answer in chorus,
sitting half-circled in their yards

beneath canopies of bougainvillaea,
amongst earthen jars of geraniums.

# Driving to the Lake

City avenues, green-bordered highways,
and then the bare dirt roads.
We bounce on stones big as cricket balls,
unroll clouds of ochre grit,
drive for an hour encountering
no person or car; watched by trees.

Aloof, motionless
as if considering the travail of growth.
Shapes that absorb the eye,
singular as cumulus.
An illusion of parkland
planted for vistas –
but these were set by winds,
by rare flushes of rain,
to stand ankled in biscuit-brown earth,
dark bronze against noon's heavy blue.

Our dust-trail hangs in the heat.
There will be coolness by the lake,
the shade of willows.

Months afterwards, in a mind
freighted with landscapes,
the eucalypts hold their ground.

# Cave Light

We glide in a soundless boat, drawn
on a route of rope across black water.
Above spreads a milky way, living
pinpoint lights dusting the cave's ceiling.

A lamp-beam's thrown; fringe upon fringe
of hanging filaments glisten from darkness,
spidersilk traps beaded with sticky drops –
the worms' aerial angling-lines.

The plumped grub pupates and is re-born,
an imago free to flit a few hours
in the vault, mouthless, bent only
on the making of new worms, new lights.

Is the worm paramount, then, that chrysalis,
wing, egg, all work towards it? Ah, but we see
perfection as the form that's most like us –
that mates, engenders young; and has to die.

# Hot Springs
*New Zealand, March 1992*


The two hens fossick along a flowerbed,
scattering crumbly soil across the grass,
propelling fallen passion-fruit –
ovoid, smooth-purple skinned –
with a sudden backward kick
a star footballer might envy.

They stroll together, tan-feathered sisters,
or rush to snip the pale green
out of hearting cabbages,
seizing the unwatched moment.

Freed battery birds, they've taken
to lawn life like ducks to a pond.
All day they converse contentedly,
continue their purring duet towards she
who picks them up to pen them.

Eggs come every day. I hold one
still core-warm, no less miraculous
than the scalding fountains that spurt
here where Earth's crust is breached,
a power latent as the roped yolks
that wait in a laying hen.

# 5 THE BOAT AT BALMAHA

# A Fable

A man who lived in a high forest
journeyed to the plain for the first time,
following his home-spring's rocky fall
until, cascades and rapids left behind,

the stream spread wide and quiet,
loitering in pools and backwaters.
One bright morning, stooping to drink,
he saw sky in the depths, and trees

and a wrinkled face rising, brown lips
pursed as if to sip the air.
He drew back, knelt further along the bank,
but the eyes of the other again

met his own – an old man, and frightened.
He need not fear me, he thought,
offering a hand. The broken surface rocked,
danced the image into wavering circles,

fragmented the green and blue. He dared
to scoop water in his palm. It was colourless,
innocent. He touched his own cheek, his brow –
could not feel the age-traced lines;

yet he knew that what the pool held
must be an echo of himself.
The homeward climb loomed difficult and long.
Would his legs carry him so far?

## Mistletoe Bough

She climbed into the box.
It was labelled THIS SIDE UP.
USE NO HOOKS. HANDLE WITH CARE.

She pulled down the four cardboard flaps.
Rumours of search filtered from above, a fret
of footsteps, calling voices. Where? Where?

Had a day gone by, she wondered, and a night?
Or a week? Time was unmeasured
while she stayed there, still and quiet.

But suddenly she feared that the house
might become silent; that she, forgotten,
might fall into solitude too deep for thought.

She saw that as the tide flows it is wise
to swim and to go on swimming,
if possible with pleasure in the strokes.

So she pushed the flaps aside, stood,
stepped out, and the box collapsed,
folded down to the floor. She groped

along the walls to the cobwebbed stair
and rose through the dark well towards
the cordial light seeping under the door.


## Montague, Capulet

Earth waits for the lark – she can't
balance up there in the air for ever –
and the juggler's muscles tire,
his somersaulting clubs fly down.

One summer day a slow covey of balloons,
carnival shapes and colours,
sailed over the city. Great bubbles
in the currents' drift they cooled,

sank down to lie along the hills
like silken portraits of themselves.

He, she, had their plans gone aright
must have come down from passion's height
and might have learned to love, stayed kind
to each other during the long pull to the tomb.

But he given to carousing, she bone-selfish —
perhaps it all happened for the best.


## The Lady and the Unicorn


Her purity deserves the finery she wears,
the small innocent fauna that surround her,
the flowers fresh and perfect
sprouting from her woollen field.

A thousand shivering sheep released
into the winds of several Springs
and many unremembered men,
hands and backbones irrevocably bent,
sight sacrificed by rushlight,
have made, strand by strand
with much skilled patience, this tribute
to her quality; honouring also
another patience, the unicorn's.

He would not presume, like Europa's bull,
to offer her his back and a rewarding
dizzy gallop towards experience. No.
His eyes upon her are bland, docile.

Almost he disowns the ridiculous pale spiral
set like an unlit candle above his mild brow.
He does not seek to kindle her maiden curiosity;
perhaps he knows nothing will.
Virginity is her profession;
she's an expert at it.


## Mater Regina


Age, sudden as frost
has embroidered upon me
the patterns of its contagion;
my stiff tread
declares it like bells.
Not for me now, nor again,
the answering flesh
the warm lips
of a young man.

I watch them, their muscled arms,
the vigour of their thighs.
They laugh from the deep ease
of their round throats
and are inaccessible to me
as the newborn are
to the long-dead.

I, Jocasta, shall not sleep again.
My bed has been my snare. The rope,
plain friend, waits undisguised
to swing me out of life, away
from my twice-loved son,
the raped face of his grief,
the fountains of red tears
that are my blood.

## Quietus Est

The crowd watched but he
could not open his eyes.
A bullock tongue
lolled from his mouth.

Pain, the weight of a blade,
drove through his belly's wall.
But he was light, light.
A voice soared castrato

in his songless throat. *I am God's
canary-bird* – he thought –
*purged for Him.* And for a moment
glory hazed the scarlet slab.

But a charnel stink
needling at lids and nostrils
stung him to bitter waking.
He saw the blood-marbled mass

tremble between labouring flames,
ash of the pyre below; dark smoke
whirling away. A welling of spittle
spilled out, his gullet crushed.

One is done, he thought, and two;
I have endured them. Now
will come the third, beyond
soul or body's bearing.

He reached within, to feel
arteries falling slack, last blood
flowing soft as wine, all gates open,
saving him.

## Pressed Man

None of them's modest, nor maidens,
and if they were, what good to us?
Draggle-dressed, gap-toothed, wild,
but they're what we need.
They weather such storms, these old tarts,
without ever leaving harbour; like gales
we bear them down flat on the planks.
The officers go ashore
(as we pressed men cannot) and I wager
are soon out of their sleek breeks
working for once as willingly as we
and at the same task, but snug
and private in a wide bed.

Time was I slept in a bed; not with a wench though.
I was twelve years old, but tall, could labour
like a man, plough like a man, the brown rump
of the mare steady before me, her tail like tresses,
the share biting the earth. A good way to live.
I remember the white seabirds
crowding in from the storm to follow me.
They would fly twenty leagues to cheat
the plovers of a few poor worms.

When the press-gang came I was working the long field,
saw the man waiting toward the furrow's end.
Would have left all, plough, horse, and run from him
but there were others beside and behind me.

In my mind old Poll still stands in the cold field
as doubtless she did that day until nightfall.
I think my father would have wept for loss of me,
loosing the harness, leading the mare home.

Harbour is what seabirds mean now
and a whore – but no foot
on land. They've made me a sailor.
I'll never have wife or roof
and, dead, shall go over the side.
The sea's belly is full of us pressed men.

# Now You See It...

If time's not a linear flow, then all
we know as dead, all those we think
have not yet taken form, share place with us,
equal tenants; but it seems plain fact
that lives move forward to their ends,
each moment ceding to the next,
all that it held consumed.

The brush fell long ago from Leonardo's hand.
Should we doubt this? Can we believe
that tender women, cracker-jawed old men,
still pose for him without rest even while
they walk in gardens, scour pots, drink
mother's milk, wait curled in the womb?

Are we each simultaneously foetus, child, dotard?
Who lives with me in this room
where I seem to be alone – and am I
here always, wherever else I go?
*When* am I, if not solely now?
The passage of time seems patent:
years serially numbered,
days defined by what we see – the sun
travelling the arc of the sky.


# Wing Walking

Wind screams in the struts,
presses with ocean strength
against chest and thighs.
The fields are a long way down,
racing and tilting; not real.

You'll show them reality!
You posture, swagger,
salute with both hands.
Waving arms far below
lift in answer.

Cruciform, the sliding shadow
brushes across toy hedges.
Suddenly the fields are too far,
the safe cockpit a world away,
the runway a lost hope.

You see at last that every step
on earth, in air, is irrevocable.


## The Year of the Dog


Of old, the princesses
would ride in palanquins
veiled to wed their unseen lords.
The matchmakers would have woven
fine threads from province to province
and by those spider-silks
bound woman to man.

We met on the train to Kew
both hungry for the same sight –
the newburst blossoms of the cherry.
Stained with the delicate flush
that dawn holds sometimes,
but only for an instant,
the snowsoft flowers breathed
their memorable perfume.

We could guess then how
under the cherry branches
the people move now, the women
with their full-grown feet
walking amongst the men.

And we, too, treading this year-long
green English grass,
could speak together
learn each other.

I shall come to him without fear
on a red palanquin
a number fourteen bus.
I shall come in my one
embroidered dress,
on my high heels.
In his small room
we shall touch,
skin against skin.
In this year of the dog
the matchmaker
has no work to do.


## The Lure


There were many who set out
each thinking himself uniquely chosen.
They rode unsquired through the wild lands
steadfast as moths drawn to a distant lure.

For, as a she-moth silently calls, the girl
untouched by any frisson of love or lust
innocently breathed out an essence
that brought them to her –

the young lords journeying in hope
with their fine lace at cuff and throat,
morocco boots and long noble faces –
second sons of wealthy or minor monarchs.

To prove themselves men and gain a kingdom
they pressed towards her spell's unravelling
through fenlands and deserts brittle with drought,
every laborious track a spoke to the hub –

136

her palace with its fabled gardens.
Each dandy prince as he approached
that lavish green would feel a new surge
of courage, her mute moth call

tugging at his will. He'd advance
dismounted, sword in hand. Alas! his blade
broke on the centenarian trees.
Their trunks rose still as sculpture

through a living weaponry of thorns and tendrils
that pierced and embraced him, lifted him
to rot and swing among the boughs.
At last one suitor, a paragon perhaps,

rode along magically subservient
avenues to wake and claim the bride.
In his embrace she spoke of hollow
uneven janglings, the only dream-sounds

of her long sleep. *It's over now*, he said;
and cut the grinning princes free,
hustled their bones into the earth –
the losers, the might-have-beens. His new crown

fitted him well, but (alas again) the princess
had lost her wits during the years of trance.
She'd sit all day fondling her childhood dolls
and could not count her fingers.


## AIDS Hospice


He phoned and told me. Now all I can do,
he said, is wait; but come and visit me.
No special hours. Ring first; sometimes I go
out for a walk when there's somebody free
to take me. Someone on the staff. You see
my balance isn't good – I might fall down.
But mostly I stay in. I watch TV
if it's a good day for my eyes. Come soon.

Edwardian brick with polished front door brass.
Beside a table littered with old crumbs
we try to talk, gaze out on rainy grass.
*The new magnolia; this year it should bloom –*
time and again his thoughts flit to the tree,
load it with blossoms he can't wait to see.


## After Stevie


I'd like to believe she'd be proud
of herself, at last in Heaven;
that she'd be comfortable on a cloud –
not hanker for Palmers Green,

a firelit room, cosy stuff-over chair,
(clouds aren't fluffy, but chilly and dank).
She'd make an unusual sort of angel – her hair
was always too straight and lank.

And do angels poke fun, tilt at convention?
She had a wicked turn of phrase –
would that merit eternal detention
in the Other Place?

No, no. So much in Hell would distress her.
The bad ones burning and screaming –
Heaven would suit her better,
a place of dreaming

where she'd often be bored I believe.
But the Lion Aunt might fly by, bringing tea and sultana bread.
So rejoice for Stevie. Do not grieve.
Death was a friend she longed for; so she said.

## The Boat at Balmaha

*(for Hilary Rutter)*


It was always in my mind there'd be a next time –
Oban or Loch Lomond on the bus,
with coffee stops and an hour on the way home
for a fill of cakes and tea in a one-street town
with time to stroll and windowshop.

Disappointment, an almost childish pang,
colours my sorrow; we'd meant to go, someday,
to the Orkneys where you were born.
That far-northern speech of yours,
soft and exact, is woven

through the fabric of my memories,
meshed with smile and stance and gesture.
It's as if you could say to me now – remember
that fine lunch, fresh steaks of salmon?
Remember the boat trip, Balmaha?

Afternoon sunshine; the still-summery trees
sketched in painterly greens and golds.
We moved out across the brown water.
Our wake streamed away, a shouldering crowd
of bubbles rising, riding, and then dispelled.


## Chavvy


It's cold in the trailer.
Can't leave them with the stove lit –
oil's murderous.
Well, they must stay in bed.
He swings into the truck,
off to Gravesend.

The boy's used to it,
whiling away the hours, talking.
Sometimes the baby listens, smiles.
Sometimes she cries. He's four,
and knows how to quieten her –
crushed biscuits soaked in milk.
He soothes her with whispers;
the roughest of rough language
falls lovingly from his lips.
His Dad will be home by teatime.
Or perhaps not.

*Who'll have them?* The radio outshouts
the diesel's beat. His head pounds
with the problem. *Silly bitch.*
*What the fuck she wanna bugger off for...*

Maggie's got five of her own
but...just for a day or two.
Play with your cousins, dear.
He squares up stylishly,
an imitative pugilist. The little girl
shows a disdain that riles him.
He snatches a breadknife.
I hold my breath; but, seven years old,
she's more than equal to him.

Later, they sit amicably on her bed
the baby asleep between them.
A bossy one, she corrects his accent,
delicately ignoring his vocabulary.
The baby wakes, cries monotonously.
Dad  dad  dad. Just a sound.

## Crying Out Loud

*(for Jacky Gillott)*

I liked the look of it on the library shelf,
the paragraphs not too long, enough dialogue,
and the writer's photograph, young, clear-eyed,
somehow familiar. It was not until later,
halfway through the book, that I remembered.

She wrote this book and had this picture taken
and, not long after, dosed herself with death.
Why were the green times of May, the open house
of summer, an irony so bitter to her
that she shut them off?

No answer in those printed eyes, gazing
at the white last page, or in the dustcover
summary: married, two sons; held jobs;
wrote novels; year and place of birth.
Not chosen then, her time and way of dying.

## Found Lines

*(Sir Walter Ralegh to his wife.*
*Death-cell, Winchester, 1603.)*

Dear Bess, I would not send you grief,
though I am no more yours, you mine.
Bear this with good heart, like thy self.

Long mourning's vain – again be wife,
since this thy husband's overthrown.
Dear Bess, I would not send you grief.

Almighty God, goodness itself,
keep thee; repose yourself in him.
Bear this with good heart, like thy self.

But for your sake I sued for life,
and for our boy's, a true man's son.
Dear Bess, I would not send you grief –

nor want, being thus surprised with death
and unresolved each debt and loan.
Bear this with good heart. Like thyself

while others sleep I watch, time's thief.
Yours that was, but not now my own,
dear Bess. I would not send you grief –
bear this with good heart, like thy self.


## A Gallery of Early Photographs


Braced, or chin on hand, or steadied
against tree-trunks or beached boats,
they were proudly willing
to stay motionless for seven minutes,
bequeathing these fixed shadows,
their uninterpreted likenesses.

Ennobled by patience,
with steadfast lips, marvellous
sad eyes, they posed for the take.
And now we take again, stare
into their nameless lives –
a smocked farmer; an old slave, creased skin
polished like Cherryblossomed leather;
whiskered industrialists in tall hats;
Chantilly brides; railway navvies;
small boys in frocks; pinafored girls;
widows with bugled bosoms.

Intimate possessions that graced
fringed mantelshelves and family pianos,
they're housed here in a conjunction
meaningless except for shared age.

A young woman caught in her distant summer
half-smiles beneath a stiffened bonnet,
holds a full rose against her cheek.
And – no parlour picture this – a soldier
lies where he's fallen, face to the earth,
perfectly still.

## Gravity

They glide across strata of air,
arms lifted and flexed,
like babies dreaming breast-down.

The camera, following, makes them seem
to drift unsinking as if, charmed swimmers,
all the time in the world is theirs –
to circle, cluster, clasp hands;
until they break, cast off, and each
at his distance releases the colours
of the sail that saves him – trusting
those air-filled arches, spread ropes;
cool in their usage.

Veteran, coaching a weekend novice,
he'd plummetted, then checked, was floating
slowly, safe as any thing can be depending
on thin air. The learner swung too near,
bumped the frail canopy. It lost its breath.

At matter's unbuoyed speed, soft and fluid,
hard and brittle, held in a thin
wrapping of skin, he dropped on a plumb-line
of narrowed strings; struck the grass.

# A Guest in the House

*(for Frances Horovitz)*

The room was low-beamed,
cavernous at dusk, I'd thought empty
until I saw the still shape of a head,
a shadow in the casement's frame
against the drained sky's grey.

She came from the window-seat
towards the deeper darkness where I stood.
A soft clear voice. *I'm Frances.*
I hear the echo of my answer,
two words: *Of course.*

Do spirits meet, life after life,
re-clothed beyond usual recognition?
It seemed that I knew her —
from that moment a good genius
in my life until hers ended, and perhaps
beyond; who knows?

# Home Is the Hunter

She's watched for his return
at each day's evening, his briefcase
stuffed as if with deermeat,
umbrella a spent spear.
Forty years of triumphal entrances,
attentive welcomings, end in this
gift-loaded euphoric homecoming.
Something near to fear

stirs in her. The house
has been hers throughout the core
of every day, close shelter
for her busy morning hours,
her re-creative afternoons.
Now it opens its traitor door,
switches allegiance to his clamour,
his masterfulness, his more

insistent needs. How long had she
dug, hoed and planted the suburban
flower-patch, made it colourful
and fragrant for his weekend
leisure? Now he comes in with the air
of a pioneer, as if her patient garden
were wilderness for his first
cultivation; and she'll pretend

(habits are hard to break) when called on
to admire, that everything he grows
is magical, as if no million years
but he alone made this summer's rose.

## The Postman Is Familiar

with everyone's letterbox. Mine's
too mean a size. For catalogues
and magazines, he rings the bell, waits,
puts the mail into my hand, and smiles.

He feeds me postcards from India,
letters from New Zealand, and is wordless;
and discreet, I'm sure. He knows
that sometimes I'm not up and dressed

by second delivery (parcels) – sees me
in dressing-gown, barefooted;
could even give evidence, if required,
as to the adequacy of my bath towel.

He knows who wears Damart and belongs to the AA,
who subscribes to Greenpeace and *Investor's News*,
who are *Readers Digest* readers and have faith
in their unique numbers that may win a Porsche.

To some he delivers names from Data-Date,
and to us all brings demands for dues, links us
to Town Halls, North Sea rigs, sewers, reservoirs
and Telecom; and turbines, however powered.

He sees red warnings through envelope windows;
knows who is sent many Christmas cards, and who none.
He remembers us each morning by number and by name,
and forgets us every afternoon.


## The Lepidopterist


The narrow room was lined with cabinets
of pale polished wood, many drawers
each shallow as a frying pan.
One at a time he pulled them forward,
exhibited the impeccably tidy corpses within –
chorus-lines of identical cream-soft virgins
and companies of camp-followers gaudy
in tortoiseshell, crimson; all noncombatants.
Some, he said, were rare.
And every one was perfect.

Hundreds. He went on showing, describing them,
making no mistakes for each was mounted
as he remembered from the years when
with clear sight he'd made
this mortuary of wings.

Blind now, he dared no longer
bring his fingers near to touch, enjoy.
Their frailty defeated him. He'd not know
whether they lay firm like pharaohs
or sank against their white cards
to spooned dust, escaping him, dead things
that on the wing had not escaped his net,
his slumberous bottle, his sharp pin.


## Semmelweiss and...


Better the gutter than the hospital
with its waiting coffins
its haunting unseen miasmas.

In the end the professor from Hungary
gave his fortune and his life
to stem the fevers and the fear.
The accoucheurs were made to wash
diligently in limewater.
Though they still worked in frockcoats –
gentlemanly breasts and skirts netted
with trails both stale and fresh
from the post-mortem room – their clean hands
brought the women through delivery
to a safe lying-in. There were fewer
anguished deaths and orphan babies.

Sometimes I dream of birth,
the crescendo of it, even the pain –
I dream pain. The place
is no labour ward I knew; the time's
not the past. I strive in a sloppy bed,
without sheets, roughly blanketed.
The light is dull, ochreous.
My stretched belly gleams, ready.
I never see the child.

[*Ignaz Philipp Semmelweis: Born Budapest 1818,
died 1865, of septicaemia*]

## Silent Head

You can see the mouth
will never utter –
feels but never...
White plaster

is blind as snow
but handwarm yet,
after the moulding,
the casting. The set

of the eyes counterfeits
sight. The straight stare
of a subject posed
is not what's here;

she looks. Her lips
search, even in dumb
whiteness seeming to tremble
as if what's to come

promises too little; or more
than head alone bargains for.


## Sleeping Pills

Sometimes, hair dressed high, she'd go
in gilded tissue to a party.
In country lanes she'd walk low-heeled,
wear rural skirts. Art was her nature.
She'd have wished even in death
to be composed for admiration,
as if in healing sleep.

The drug betrayed her, drew
her sinews tight, bruised, warped,

stiffened her body as it strained
and sucked for the last hope of air
though she'd already sunk
where air was not. Her will
had meant to die, had made it sure.

But if she'd known how ugly
her chosen death's particular stamp
might she have closed the bottle,
brushed her hair,
gone down to make some tea?

They found her, dark as the bog-buried girl
whose crone-face brought to shaming light
mocked with a leathern grin
the loss of rose and white.


## Smiling

The young men wear white flannels to play
cricket on the beach while the girls
(flappers I suppose) sit under sunshades
against seaweedy wooden breakwaters
drinking something from thermos cups.

*Click!* shingle, low-water sand,
bundled children paddling at the wave-edge.
*Click!* swimmers, bathing-beauty posers,
dozing elders cautiously clothed...
Everyone eyes-front as *Click!*

they smile towards the smiling
Kodak girl in her breezy zebra-frock,
enjoying the summer and new liberty –
war shooed away, the blood
and the trenches plastered over.

Their smiles seem unworried, confident;
but so do ours when playtime cameras
record us – carefree, smiling.

## Summer Festival

Amongst all the huckstering, the heat,
the slapstick, dramas and musical
excitements, the curries, pizzas and warm
wine, there's one thing I remember best –

the prize-giving on Friday night, an event
of private pleasures rivalled only
by Sunday evening's spectacular,
the Magic Lantern Show.

Who'd have thought buildings could burn
and ships sink before your very eyes by means
merely of three-inch circles of painted glass
manipulated in a beam of light?

Who'd have imagined the plain screen,
that covered the whole wall of the high room,
would suddenly pulse with colour, rich vortices
and brilliant arabesques merging

and dissolving and always symmetrical,
an abstract ballet so absorbing that for an hour
I forgot everything, even the prize-giving,
though that had had its rhythms too,

its patterns, its intangible rewards –
laurels not to be worn, rainbow trophies
that would stand on no proud shelf;
only this, a riddle, for its record.


## Trust

Years later, moved at last to tell,
my daughter talks of being lost
after midnight, running blindly
along dark dockyard streets,
a car drawing to the kerb.

150

She feels a frisson of fear even now
remembering how that younger self
slipped into the seat, thankful
to be helped towards rendezvous
and a safe conduct home.

We might not be together now
in a summer garden – so she thinks,
hearing of Lynne Rogers, a girl
offered what seemed the chance
of a good job – an interview arranged;
not in a room with a telephone,
an ushering secretary,
but in the noise and rush
of a railway terminus.
Naïve, it seems afterwards,
not to have doubted.

She travelled alone to the meeting,
brought, as instructed, her passport.


## The Widower


The old man is in mourning for his wife,
re-walking her paths, pacing the house
as if gathering into himself
perceptions that have been hers.
His glance rests along her dead glance
like hand upon hand.
And he, a clergyman, thinks of her not
as a being without flesh, alive forever,
but as the bodily leaver of fingerprints
that will now day by day be overlaid
on cup, pew, doorknob.

The bereaved have to bear two faces.
It can't be seen, in a crowd, who they are –
carrying within them a grey protoplasm
that drags at the ribcage, won't take

any comfortable shape.
Their real lips are not those that smile
but those that kiss a page of handwriting;
that in the night hours beseech
the bedroom air, where not a molecule
of flesh resides, to return an answer,
against all certitude.

He seeks her not as a translated soul
but here amongst the furniture;
seeks her as ghost and oracle –
no surer than those less primed
of her place elsewhere.


## Young Woman Powdering Herself
*(Seurat, 1890)*


Look long, and she might seem
to lift that soft left hand, or slowly
begin to rise from whatever stool or tuffet...
But the heavy sand-sweeps of her skirt

detain her, hold her firm – an icon
drifted with the colours of the shore
dusts of garnet, zircon, topaz,
scruples of iron ore, tourmaline.

The painter's alter ego, precise, discreet,
or the most sensual of mistresses? Unlaced,
she'd be sister to a Rubens paramour –
breasts that might lull obsession, absorb

the nicety of coloured mote and speck
into the wholeness of warm flesh.
Flesh; but she's enamelled, finite,
a casket for secrets.

She powders, perfumes herself for him,
for their enclosed room – she'll not join
the Sunday promenaders strolling across
new-green grasses soaked in light.

152

# 6  AS IF FOR EVER

## Reflections in a Hotel Room

Mirror, mirror on the wall
who is this person? She's older
than she who lives with me,
the one always on call

behind the kinder mirrors at home.
This one is top lit. A hard strip
of sheathed brilliance, more merciless
than an old-style star's wreath

of yellow tungsten bulbs,
strokes definition into blue-brown
smears beneath her eyes, deepens
the scored lines that record

a lifetime of emotions
seldom disguised. Why, look!
At this very moment, tears
spill from her stupid eyes.


## Menopause

Moods' ebb and flow ruled
by bright or clouded days,
not by the forceful womb.

Belly will not grow round again
unless, like a man's, from excess;
but not unsexed, not done with love.

Invisibly new-seasoned.
Long vassaldom served through.
Self, while the light lasts.

## Cinderella

Years
hang on me like rags;
no Godmother can dress me again
in smooth silk.

Though I sit at the spent hearth
I am your sister.
I am the dream
the ride
the dance
the idyll.

Proud lovely girls
look deep.
See, I am seventeen
inside.


## Skin

It was sheer silk once, silk
from toe to brow; is as fine now
only in the smooth hollow
between collarbone and breast.
Tucked into my shrugged shoulder
my cheek browses
for the linger of perfection.

Ah, Helen! Were you lifted flawless
to the stars, or did you live on,
vulnerable to time, answered
by mirrors? Did truth gaze back
from some unruffled pool, or bathing
as became your state in marble's
luxurious lap, did you see

with sad acknowledgement
the crêpe-de-chine of hands
and forearms, the change from smooth
to slack no ointment could reverse?

And seeing, did you fear
there might be no more love?


## For Kay Whicher
*(9 May 1920 – 14 May 1990)*


She's set deep in the years' amber,
brownhaired girl in a WAAF billet. Laughing,
half-dressed in shirt and sheeny bloomers,
she slaps a firm thigh in a parody of pantomime –
'Off to the woods, my merry men!'

Lost touch, then an encounter – it might so easily
have been a near miss – in the doorway of a café;
Westminster, where neither of us lived.
By then we had husbands, she a daughter;
and we were both newly pregnant.

They'd be May births. It was like summer,
the day she went into labour.
I remember my heavy self sitting to rest
on some cool museum's bench – but nothing
of where it was, my mind bemused,

imagining white walls, high viewless windows,
the cloistered, inescapable, struggle; she
in the throes of experience as yet not mine.
I'd read books, practised for painless birth,
guessed it might be less easy.

Our sons, now older by more than a decade
than we were, bearing them, have met
only as children. After so long a silence
what prompted my sudden search, enquiry
about her whereabouts from friends,

the urgent need to phone? The next day,
she said, she was to go to hospital.
From the lightness of her voice I conjured
another ward, flowers, warmth, a getting well.
She, though, had known what was to come.

## Old Scholars

The first was a girl; she'd been
tennis champion, glossy-haired
school idol. She vanished
of a fast consumption.

And then the boys began dying.
Edwards, Mitchell, Williams,
Dawson, Ross, dead in wrecked planes,
in floating dinghies found too late,
or choking on sand, on blood.
Graham died from marching, a prisoner,
his quick brain no help against hardship.

It's beginning again; coronaries, cancer.
Another battle order, a mounting
casualty list.

## Old Age

We squat under olive trees, washing shards.
The mule watches from another shade.

Did he carry me here?  No, I'm sure
we all racketed through the village
and up the hill in an old jeep.
There's no dust where we sit; grey-green

shields us, our hats are on the grass
awaiting our next foray into the heat.
The heat o' the sun. I hold it in my bones
at the moment of waking.

Now I dream continually of countries
I shall never see, or not come to again
except in my untiring mind. Memory
and projection are ravelled, one.

The mule is so real he stamps, stares,
nods his shaved muzzle. Aureoles of light
gild the heads of my companions.
They're young, bent to their work.

What do they see when they glance up
and I am there?

## As If For Ever

Poor dead; the maiden
has them under the ice.
The fissures they slipped through
are sealed over. Like iron plates
the ice has covered them in.
They bob unseen, hunched shapes
nudging the implacable ceiling.

The skaters come,
we among them carrying our lanterns
and the moon rises. The lake
is wreathed in her white smile
and we all skate as if for ever.